Simple Secrets to a Beautiful Home

Emilie Barnes

HARVEST HOUSE PUBLISHERS

EUGENE, OREGON

Cover by Garborg Design Works, Minneapolis, Minnesota

SIMPLE SECRETS TO A BEAUTIFUL HOME
Formerly *The Spirit of Loveliness*
Copyright © 1992 by Harvest House Publishers
Published by Harvest House Publishers
Eugene, Oregon 97402
www.harvesthousepublishers.com

Library of Congress Cataloging-in-Publication Data

Barnes, Emilie.
  [Spirit of loveliness]
  Simple secrets to a beautiful home / Emilie Barnes.
     p. cm.
Originally published: The spirit of loveliness. c1992.
Includes bibliographical references.
  ISBN 0-7369-0969-9 (pbk.)
  1. Women—Spiritual life. 2. Women—Conduct of life. I. Title.
  BV4527.B3588 2004
  248.8'43—dc22

                                                    2003015761

Printed in the United States of America.

  04   05   06   07   08   09   10   11   12   /BP-KB /   10   9   8   7   6   5   4   3   2   1

Contents

To Jenny, my daughter,
and to Christine, my granddaughter.

May your lives be filled with the
Spirit of God, and may he produce in
each of you beauty that will bless your homes
and those who live in them and visit them.

An Invitation

*P*lease come in—to my home and to the pages of this book. I only wish you could really visit and share a cup of tea. We could lean back on the sofa cushions, nibble a cookie, and talk.

Talk about what? About home. Not necessarily "house beautiful," but a home filled with simple beauty. About my home, which I love, and which I love to share with others. And about your home—and you. For I talk with hundreds of women like you every month, and I truly believe you have a heart for home.

Your life situation may not be like mine. Maybe you're newly married, just starting out in a tiny apartment with a sprinkling of furniture and a few wedding presents. Maybe you live in a simple tract home with a struggling lawn, a few baby trees, and a houseful of little kids. Maybe you're single, in a suburban condo with security patrol and silent neighbors, or maybe you've just moved to a much smaller place after the kids have left home. Maybe your home is just a room in somebody else's house!

Your taste may not be like mine. You may prefer clean, modern lines to the chintz and china that I love. Maybe you can't live without a piano and wall-to-wall bookshelves. You may prefer chunky pottery mugs to the dainty china cups I collect.

But if you're like the women I meet in my seminars and through my mail, you long for a home that is warm and welcoming, comfortable and freeing—a place where you can express the uniqueness of your God-given talents and nurture relationships with people you love. You are hungry for a home—and a life—that reflects your personality and renews your soul. I hope this book will help your heart shine forth beautifully wherever you live and wherever you go.

—Emilie Barnes

Chapter 1

Welcome is what reflects
God's spirit of love, joy,
and happiness.

—EMILIE BARNES

The Secret of Welcome

*W*elcome home!

That's what I want my life to say to everyone whose path crosses mine. I want to create an atmosphere of serenity and joy, of blessing and belonging, that embraces people (myself included) and draws them in—an atmosphere that makes them feel loved and special and cared for.

I'll never forget my excitement more than 48 years ago when my husband, Bob, carried me over the threshold of our first apartment. It had just three tiny rooms, but it felt like a castle to us. Bob was a first-year teacher, fresh from college. I was a 17-year-old child bride, still in my last year of high school, still working for my mother in her little dress shop. We were so proud of our very first home, and we put our hearts and souls into making it a comfortable and inviting place.

Together we sprayed white paint on an old wrought-iron lawn table someone had given us, creating a dainty but sturdy dining table. I sewed pink eyelet curtains for the windows while Bob spray-painted egg cartons to glue on the walls for a "white-on-white" texture. We had one canvas chair, a box for a lamp table, and an old trunk for a coffee table. But we found great joy in living there together and sharing our apartment with others.

After our children had left the nest, and after a progression of condos and tract homes, we crossed the threshold of the converted barn where we spent many wonderful years. We saw such potential in that lovely old house—the hardwood floors, the high-ceilinged "great room," the kitchen with its dozens of cupboards and cabinets, the tree-covered grounds. And we had so much fun remodeling and redecorating and landscaping to make it ours.

Unfortunately, due to my recent cancer treatment, we had to sell the "Barnes Barn" and change our style of decorating. One difference in our lives is that Bob no longer has to care for all our acreage. Instead, we are now adapting to a wonderful, relaxing beach lifestyle. And we're finding that we love our new home as much as we have loved our previous homes.

What we were doing in our dream house and now in our beach house is really no different from what we had done in that little apartment years before. It is no different from what you do in *your* house or apartment or condominium.

We are homemaking—literally "making a home." We are working to create a lifestyle that says "welcome" to ourselves and everyone around us.

The Meaning of Home

Why is a "welcome home" lifestyle so important? I truly believe we all need a spiritual center, a place where we belong. A place where we can go to unwind and regroup and get in touch with who we truly are...and then reach out to share with others.

That doesn't necessarily mean a physical location. Home is as much a state of the heart and spirit as it is a specific place. Many a person living on the road has learned to "make herself at home" in hotel rooms, other people's houses, or wherever she finds herself.

And yet...just as our spirits require physical bodies to do God's work here on earth, most of us need a physical place we can call home. And we have the privilege of making the place where we live into a welcoming refuge for ourselves and others—a place where simplicity and beauty can find a foothold in our lives.

This kind of home doesn't take a lot of money or even a lot of time. (I've seen it done by stay-at-home moms and high-placed executives and even a just-graduated bachelor or two.) It doesn't require a professional's touch in decorating or cooking or home maintenance. It can certainly be done without a maid.

What a welcoming home *does* require is a caring and willing spirit—a determination to think beyond bare-bones necessities and to make room in our lives and schedules and budgets for what pleases the senses and enriches the soul. Most of all, it requires an "I can" attitude, a confidence that we have something to share and the ability to share it.

That special sense of "I can" is what I hope you find in this book. Along with sharing some simple, practical secrets for making "welcome home" a way of life, I want to inspire you and give you hope. As you read these pages, I hope they touch the spirit of loveliness that lives within you and motivate you to make whatever changes you need to develop a spirit of welcome in your life. Let's get started.

A Safe Refuge

A welcoming home is a place of refuge, a place where people worn down by the noise and turmoil and hostility of the outside world can find a safe resting place. A welcoming home is a place that you and others enjoy coming home to.

If you live in a house with small children, you may already be shaking your head. "What do you mean, 'noise and turmoil of the outside world'? I have to *leave* home to get away from noise and turmoil!"

> *May its doors be open to those in need, and its rooms be filled with kindness. May joy shine from its windows, and His presence never leave it.*
>
> —JEWISH HOME BLESSING

But even in the rough-and-tumble of family living, home can be a safe haven and even a place of quiet (at least some of the time). And *especially* if noise and activity crowd your life, making the extra effort to create a sense of refuge in the middle of it can pay off wonderful dividends.

Besides, a refuge is not a hole where you disappear to eat and sleep and then emerge to go about the business of life. A welcoming home is where real life happens. It's where personalities are nurtured, where growth is stimulated, where people feel free not only to be themselves but also to develop their best selves. That caring, nurturing quality—not the absence of noise or strife—is what makes a home a refuge.

Single people, in fact, may need to make a special effort to cultivate the welcome in their environment. If you live alone, it's easy to fall into the "hole" mentality and deprive yourself of the spiritual and emotional benefits of a welcoming home.

Writer Andrea Wells Miller learned the value of welcome-home living during her single days, after coming home from a business trip to her empty apartment:

> As I looked around, only my ivy plant looked back. The pillows on the sofa, the bedroom slippers out of place and askew on the floor,

> the dusty end table with a dirty coffee cup on
> it, all reminded me that I was alone. No one
> had bothered anything while I was away.
> Everything was just as I had left it.
>
> I went the short distance from the entry hall to
> the kitchen. Everything was neat and clean,
> except the coffee percolator sitting alone on
> the cabinet....I opened the lid and looked
> inside—green moldy splotches were floating
> on the half-inch of coffee I had not poured
> out. It amazed me how quickly mold could
> grow.[1]

Andrea learned to counteract that "empty apartment" feeling by making a few changes. She plugged her lamp and radio into a wall socket connected to the light switch by the door. That way, one flip of a switch brought lights and music. She also made a point, when possible, of cleaning up ahead of time, leaving fresh towels, fresh sheets, and a clean coffeepot. "Those little touches helped me feel warm and welcomed when I returned from a trip."[2]

As Andrea discovered, it doesn't take much to make home feel like a refuge. Soft light—lamps, candlelight, or even firelight—rather than a harsh overhead glare. Soothing music. Something bright or pretty near the door to greet visitors and homecomers. Pleasant fragrances: scented candles, potpourri, spices boiling on the stove, or—most powerful of all—dinner in the oven. Taking just five minutes to straighten the vestibule and light a welcoming candle can make a huge contribution to making your home a welcoming sanctuary for anyone who steps inside.

A Sense of Order

A welcoming home has a sense of order about it. Not stiff, stultifying order that goes to pieces over a speck of dust or that sacrifices relationships in the interest of cleanliness, but a comforting, confident sense that life is under control. A sense that people, not possessions, are in charge of the household, that emotions are expressed but never used as weapons, that life is proceeding with a purpose and according to an overall plan.

A welcoming home is organized around the purpose of making life easier and more meaningful. Its physical tidiness frees us to enjoy the beauty in our surroundings and concern ourselves about more important matters than unearthing a clean shirt or battling an infestation of roaches.

And yes, I'm talking about cleaning house. I'm also talking about goal setting, time management, family negotiations—but not as ends in themselves. In a truly welcoming home, organization takes its proper place in the overall scheme of the universe. The daily chores of maintenance become something we can glory in, partly because they don't overwhelm us or define our whole existence.

Most of us respond positively to that kind of order in our lives because we are made in the image of God, and because God organized the whole universe to proceed in an orderly fashion. Think of the creation, when God created a beautiful, populated globe out of darkness and chaos. He is the ultimate Organizer, and the results of his ordering Spirit are always good. We automatically feel more comfortable and more welcome when we sense his kind of order in our lives.

But don't let this talk of order and organization make you feel guilty or panicked. Even if chaos and clutter in your home and life are wearing you down, the solution is not a whirlwind effort to "get organized." Unless you begin with the heart, the most complete reorganization of house and home will just give you a clean slate for chaos—and may drive you and everyone else crazy in the process.

We humans weren't made to "get organized." We were made to live as God's children, worshiping him and delighting in him. As we open our hearts and attitudes to God, putting him first in our lives and looking to him for guidance, he will show us little ways to organize the chaos and lead a more peaceful, ordered existence.

And it doesn't have to happen all at once. It has taken me 30 years to develop the systems that help me maintain order and a sense of welcome in my life—and I'm still learning. I only hope that God will use this book to bring you a little closer to a sense of comforting order and welcoming beauty.

An Expression of You

Here's another unmistakable mark of a welcoming home: It's an expression of *you*. A welcoming home is one that reflects the spirit and personalities of the people who make it. This means that if your home and your life look and feel just like mine, one of us has a problem. Your home should be uniquely and beautifully *you*.

If you live with other people, making your house an expression of you certainly doesn't mean you can't take your family or roommate's tastes into account. A welcoming home is a reflection of *everyone* who lives there. Part of its charm is the sense of diverse personalities merging to create a unique environment. Your music stand, your husband's Audubon prints, and your son's baseball trophy *can* peacefully coexist. Together, they can speak a welcome to anyone who visits.

Zoning laws, landlords' rules, and your neighbors' feelings might also limit some of your impulses toward self-expression. I once read about a woman in Houston who, with her son, built an entire house out of recycled beverage cans. In most neighborhoods, such a bizarre endeavor might spoil a few relationships!

Still, if you take seriously the privilege and responsibility of making a home, the home you make will be a unique and personal expression. The welcome it extends is the welcome you extend in your own life.

In addition, of course, the welcome *is* you. The spirit of welcome begins in your own heart, in your own attitudes. It has its birth in your willingness to accept yourself as God's child and to be grateful for your place in God's family, your true spiritual home. With that foundation, welcome becomes a way of life. You open your life to others instead of shutting them out. You treasure your close relationships for what they are—gifts from God. With that attitude, a smile and a hug become as important to the spirit of welcome as a candle and a pot of stew.

A Blessing

Most important, a welcoming home is a place of blessing—a place where you are made aware of God's blessing and through which you pass on his blessings to others.

Bob and I have always believed that our home belongs to God, not to us. In fact, six weeks after we moved into our Barnes Barn, we paid homage to that fact with a house blessing. Our church family shared dinner on the grounds. Then we stood together with our pastor for a little ceremony dedicating the property to God. Before we spent our first night in our barn, I walked into each room and prayed a blessing upon its walls, asking that peace, joy, love, honesty, and patience would permeate the surroundings.

We believe that God honored our request, for that house was a rich source of blessing to us and to others. From that day when we stood on the grounds and gave it back to God, we had dinners, Bible studies, seminars, and many other gatherings on the grounds.

Best of all were the weddings—especially the gala reception for our own son, Brad, and his bride, Maria. The weather on that July day in 1990 was perfect—85 degrees, with breezes blowing in the trees as the music surrounded the 400 guests. Brad and Maria were transported from the church a block away in a beautiful carriage behind a white horse who clippity-clopped down tree-lined Rumsey Drive onto our grounds. It was truly an occasion to remember. And as we gathered to celebrate the establishment of a new household, it was a wonderful time to remember the whole point of home.

For home is not merely a structure of wood, brick, and metal. Home is what grows within its walls, nurtured by the hearts and souls of those who live within. Allow the joy and peace of our Lord to permeate the walls of your home and the "rooms" of your life with a spirit of welcome that only Christ himself can give you. Open your heart and allow your teachable spirit to develop a home and a life that are filled with caring, warmth, and genuine hospitality.

Simple Secrets

- ❧ What do you see first when you walk through your door? If you do nothing else in a day, make sure the entry area is clean and beckoning.

- ❧ Hang a bright banner by your door to say hello to everyone who comes—or try painting your door bright red!

- ❧ Don't be afraid to fill your home with what *you* like. And everything doesn't have to match. A mix of colors, textures, and styles can be a charming expression of who you are.

- ❧ A gentle, modulated voice does wonders for making those around you feel loved and welcome. Screaming rarely accomplishes anything besides making everyone feel stressed.

❧ Fresh flowers are such an inexpensive way of saying welcome. You don't need a dozen roses from the florist. A bunch of daisies from the supermarket, an iris from your yard, or even a handful of dandelions from the curb can proclaim, "Love lives here."

❧ Flowers don't need to be confined to vases. My gifted daughter, Jenny, graced the tops of our bureaus and armoires with a beautiful tangle of silk flowers and plants. Her arrangements added such a special touch to our high-ceilinged "great room."

❧ If there are small children in your life, think of ways to make your life "childfriendly" as well as "childproof." Tuck a basket of children's books and toys in a corner, and toss a few throw pillows beside it to make a welcoming place to play.

❧ Does your telephone voice speak a welcome? Is it warm, helpful, and gracious? Does it represent a sweet spirit to people who call? (The same goes for your answering machine message.)

❧ Family photos are such an easy way of welcoming others into your life. A collection of small pictures in a variety of interesting frames will spark up any corner. If you have old portraits of Great-Grandma or Uncle Ed, don't hide them in a drawer; share them with your family and your guests.

❧ When you travel, plan ahead to take "home" with you. A clock radio, family pictures, or a "prayer basket" with Bible, prayer organizer, and flowers can help you make a welcoming home away from home.

❧ Monitor the noise levels around you, and do what you can to turn down the decibels. Instead of letting the TV blare, turn on some soft music. Or turn off all the plugged-in sound and sing your own song.

❧ Marinate a cut-up chicken (pieces or quartered) in fresh orange juice, two cloves of crushed garlic, sliced ginger root, and one tablespoon

Worcestershire sauce. Bake slowly for two hours at 250 degrees until done. What a wonderful, welcoming aroma—and dinner to boot!

❧ Light a candle by the kitchen sink. The soft light can add a touch of loveliness even to a tub of greasy water and a messy counter.

❧ Sometime during an evening at home, take a few minutes to go into the bedrooms and turn down the sheets. Borrow a welcoming idea from fine hotels and leave a chocolate or a little sachet on the pillow.

❧ Parsley in a jar of water in the refrigerator looks inviting to those who open it. I also enjoy keeping a "bouquet" of parsley on the windowsill by the sink.

❧ Cross-stitch or hand-letter (or commission from a talented friend) a blessing to hang by your front door *on the inside* so it speaks to you, your family, and your guests as you go out into the world: "The Lord bless you and keep you; the Lord make his face shine upon you and be gracious to you; the Lord turn his face toward you and give you peace."

Chapter 2

*Creativeness in the world is,
as it were, the eighth day
of creation.*

—Nikolai Berdyaev

The Secret of Creativity

I've heard it a million times—expressed with admiration and usually a little envy: "Oh, she's so creative."

Usually these words describe an "artsy" kind of person—someone who paints or writes or makes pottery. Such creative pursuits can bring great joy to those who do them and to those who enjoy the results. But you really don't have to be an artist to infuse your home and life with the benefits of creativity.

Creativity is a God-given ability to take something ordinary and make it into something special. It is an openness to doing old things in new ways and a willingness to adapt other people's good ideas to suit our personal needs. And creativity is an ability we all possess, although many of us keep it hidden in the deep corners of our lives.

Every single human being is creative. The creative spirit is part of our heritage as children of the One who created all things. And nurturing our creativity is part of our responsibility as stewards of God's good gifts.

Creative Seeing

Creativity is so much more than "arts and crafts." It is a way of seeing, a willingness to see wonderful possibilities in something unformed or ordinary or even ugly.

The first year Bob and I moved to Riverside, California, we went to an auction in an old building near Mount Rubidoux. It was fun to see the various "treasures" that were up for sale—everything from armoires to yarn caddies—and to listen as the auctioneer shouted the calls. Then an old, greasy market scale went up—and Bob shouted a bid. I nearly died on the spot. Whatever did he think we would do with *that?*

We won the bid and paid $32 for that ugly old scale. When we went to pick it up, I looked at it doubtfully, but Bob was sure he had bought a treasure. He was right! We stripped the old scale clean, shined and polished it until it almost looked new, and put it on a table. That was more than 20 years ago, and we are still enjoying Bob's imaginative purchase. It graces the narrow table behind our sofa with fruit in the tray—or sometimes a pot of flowers, a bowl of potpourri, or a Boston fern. Over the years, as we continue to shop for antiques, we often see scales not nearly as nice as ours that cost hundreds of dollars. I am so grateful to Bob for his creative input into our home.

One day Bob brought me another treasure from one of his antique sprees. It was a large, wooden, hand-carved, rectangular bowl—another of those "What will I ever do with that thing?" items. But how I enjoy that bowl as it sits on our butcher block island in the center of our kitchen! I keep it full of potatoes, onions, avocados, oranges, lemons, apples, and a variety of other fruits and vegetables. It's not only beautiful, but very practical—another example of Bob's "creative seeing."

A Heritage of Creativity

The kind of vision that brings the special out of the ordinary has long been part of the American tradition. Even in the tiniest frontier cabin, pioneer women found ways to express their creative urges and to add touches of loveliness to their environment.

In great-grandma's day, quilting was a wonderfully creative pursuit for women in many areas of the country. When women married or had a baby, friends and families gathered together to make the quilts they needed to keep warm. They used old, discarded clothing, cut up and patched together into colorful designs and then carefully padded and stitched to make warm coverings. The women worked, talked, and exchanged recipes; they solved garden, food, husband, and children problems all while their hardworking fingers sewed. These quilts were truly labors of love—practical coverings transformed from simple materials and a basic household need into a work of art and an occasion for celebration.

> *We cannot make something where nothing existed— whether it be a poem, a house, or a painting— without breathing life into it so that it may itself breathe.*
>
> —ELIZABETH O'CONNOR

The "More Hours in My Day" seminars that Bob and I conduct have taken us several times to the state of Ohio, the home of many Mennonite and Amish people. Amish women still gather daily to quilt and to visit, and they have gorgeous, bright coverlets to show for their work. The spirit of creativity flourishes in their simple, homespun tradition.

Quilts are priceless examples of folk art and a beautiful testimony to the creativity of our American heritage. Where I live, they are making a huge comeback. Even the million-dollar homes in our area are decorating their beds and sofas with quilts. And each of the high, old-fashioned beds in our own home proudly displays a hand-stitched Amish quilt. (Other quilts drape an antique quilt rack or are stacked under a table.) When I look at them, I am filled with a sense of reverence for the gift of creativity they represent.

But the "quilt revival" is far more than a decorating trend; it is a living art. Many women are not only buying quilts, but rediscovering the joy of making them. Right here in our state of California there are numberless quilting classes, quilting groups, and quilting guilds. People are rediscovering the fulfilled and homey wholesomeness of the days when women gathered to pool their creativity and beautify their homes with warmth and comfort.

Something Special

Quilting is not the only creative secret you can use to enrich your life and home. The womanly tradition of making ordinary objects serve double duty as things of beauty is alive and well in many households and is constantly expressing itself in new ways.

The first time I used a bedsheet as a tablecloth, for instance—quite a few years ago—everyone thought it was a cute idea, but a little strange. Sheets were made to put on beds, not tables. But now sheets are used for curtains, drapes, sofa cushions, ironing board covers, quilts, wallpaper, placemats, napkins, windowshades, and much, much more. The fabric is wonderful—easy to wash, never needs ironing, folds well, and stacks smoothly—and one sheet provides a wide expanse of seamless material. The prices are great if you watch for sales and shop outlets and discount stores, and the variety of patterns is astounding. Even catalogs offer sheets in beautiful, feminine prints and florals.

My friend Lynn took Ralph Lauren sheets that she bought on sale and decorated her entire house in the same print—a beautiful blue floral. She covered two sofas, softened her windows with billows of sheets, made dozens of throw pillows. She lined an antique armoire with the sheets and put in shelves, a pretty crystal lamp, and all her dishes and special memory pieces. The table had a runner in the same print with a centerpiece of silk flowers in the same floral colors. In her kitchen she backed her cupboards with a blue pillow ticking strip. (Who would think of fabric in kitchen cupboards except Lynn's own creative spirit?)

It really takes very little besides creativity to turn our homes, condos, and apartments into true retreats—bits of heaven on earth. The world around us can be changed by the smallest of creative touches. The woman who takes time to think creatively can put together a homey environment out of whatever she has.

Cost, size, and possessions really have little to do with a beautiful home. In fact, if we own too much, we can easily let our lives degenerate to the point that we are merely a keeper of things. (I heard a great saying: "Life is 5 percent joy, 5 percent grief, and 90 percent maintenance.") In many cases, the loveliest things are also the simplest.

Another friend of mine, Irene, moved with her husband, Dan, to a small village in the mountains where Dan pastored a small church. We visited them and experienced what Irene had done to a tiny mountain cabin full of "inherited" wicker furniture. Irene painted all the old wicker white. Then she hit the sheet aisle of the local discount stores. Soon plump, colorful cushions brightened the wicker chairs and sofas. Adorable matching drapes covered the windows. The bedroom wall was papered with sheets. So was the bathroom—and the shower curtain was also a sheet. For less than a hundred dollars, Irene turned a dingy cabin into a dreamy retreat for the two of them.

And then something even more exciting began to happen for Irene. Encouraged by friends who visited and praised her decorating talents, Irene decided to take a few classes and eventually became an interior designer. She also teaches "Do It Yourself with What You Have" seminars out of her home, where she encourages women to make their homes into beautiful blessings. A wonderful career and ministry have grown out of Irene's willingness to use her God-given creative talents to transform what she had into something lovely.

The Joy of Creating

As wonderful as the results of our creativity can be, beautiful results are not the only benefit we receive when we're willing to be creative. The act of creating, of making beauty out of something ordinary, brings joy in itself. Watching a brightly colored afghan emerge from a basket of yarn or a beat-up old table do a Cinderella act under the "magic wand" of a paintbrush can be incredibly fulfilling— and a spruced-up den is a wonderful extra. The fun of serving brunch on miscellaneous but perfectly matched pottery and linens is second only to the creative fun of finding the plates at a garage sale, the cups at a local discount store, the tablecloth (a sheet) on a clearance table at J.C. Penney's, and the napkins (another sheet) in the back of my linen closet.

Contrary to what some people think, creativity doesn't have to be totally original. Picking up ideas from books or magazines or borrowing a brainstorm from a friend are not "cheating." In fact, creativity stimulates more creativity. The more ideas you collect from the outside, the more creative you will be in adapting those ideas and coming up with different ones of your own.

When we lived in our "barn," one of the things our guests liked most about our dining room was the hundreds of baskets that hung from the ceiling. Each basket was different—some were willow, some wicker, some twig; some with a sprig of dried flowers tucked in. All together, they picked up the charm of the aged bricks that formed the floor of the room and relaxed the more formal effect of table and china cabinet. I saw that idea first in a magazine, but for a very different room. It was exciting to see how nicely it worked in our dining room.

Even in borrowing someone else's idea, it is almost impossible to keep from making a creative endeavor your own. My longtime friend Rosemary, has a shell and rock collection. That's far from an original idea, but Rosemary has used it to preserve memories of their many travels around the world. On all their trips, she collected shells and pretty rocks from places they visited. And her treasures show up everywhere in her home: in jars, vases, bowls, and around their plants outdoors. She has even hot-glued them around picture and mirror frames, creating wonderful conversation pieces as well as things of beauty.

Another friend, Yoli, has added a musical ring to the basic idea of creative expression through collections: She collects bells. Many of her bells have come to her as gifts from all over the country. She displays them on a round lamp table in their living room and can tell a special story about each one. It's so fun to ring them and listen to the different sounds, from the tiniest crystal tinkler to a huge, loud dinnerbell.

Creative Sharing

Creativity is not just for self-fulfillment. Much of the joy of creativity comes in sharing it with others. We learned that truth first as children as we crayoned masterpieces for people we loved. And we still experience the joy of creating and sharing when we cross-stitch a Scripture for a friend, write up a recipe for a new acquaintance, or hand-letter a special card for a coworker who has been promoted.

Once when I was recovering from surgery, a dear friend, Ginny, shared her creativity with me in a very special way. She showed up in my hospital room with a "recovery kit" for the twelve days after my operation. In a pretty basket nestled twelve separately wrapped gifts labeled "Day 1," "Day 2," "Day 3," and so on.

Among the items that I so appreciated during those painful days were a sweet card, a refrigerator magnet, a puzzle to keep me very busy, a bag of potpourri, a can of chicken soup, a jar of "bubble-stuff" to blow away my misery, an apple to help keep the doctor away, an audiotape to keep me singing and happy, some Chapstick to keep my lips well moistened as I played "show and tell" about my surgery, funny cards and cartoons to make me laugh (very carefully, so I wouldn't pop a stitch!), "thank you" stickers to brighten up my letters, a cookie cutter, and some candy. What fun and friendship Ginny and I shared along with the gift of her creativity—which, of course, was really the gift of herself.

A Legacy of Joy

One of the most valuable ways we can share the secret of creativity is by modeling it for our children. We give them a legacy of joy when we teach them to use their own God-given creativity to instill beauty into their own lives and homes.

When we moved into our Barnes Barn, our daughter, Jenny, and her husband bought our two-story home. The house was dark and very country—not at all their look. At that time funds were quite tight for this young couple, and yet they felt it was important to set aside a small redecorating budget. Together they stripped wallpaper and painted all the rooms white. What a transformation took place! The house looked larger, brighter, and happier. Sheets in solids and florals became valances in all the rooms. The dark living room shutters, also painted white, took on an open, airy look.

Jenny took birch tree branches and formed them into wreaths. She added dried and silk flowers, twisted ribbon about, and had beautiful, feminine pieces of art to embellish the fireplace and hang over the bed. Bright bedspreads from a sale catalog transformed the children's rooms into cheerful places to play and dream.

As I watched Jenny work to transform that little house, I rejoiced to see her God-given creativity translated into a warm, happy environment for the people I love. Today Jenny and her family live in another house which her special creative touch has transformed into a home. And she is passing along the gift of creativity, just as she learned it from Bob and me. These days I love to see our granddaughter, Christine, use her creativity to decorate her own room, using resources she has at hand to make her environment into a welcoming, original place.

Women over the ages have used their creativity to fill their homes and lives with beauty. But creativity in the home is by no means limited to women. Our son, Brad, two years out of college, found a real dump of a duplex in Manhattan Beach, California. He went into partnership with a college friend and bought the property. They planned to live in half of the duplex and rent out the back unit.

From our point of view, those boys had paid far too much money for such dilapidated property, even if it was two blocks from the beach. It was hard for us even to think creatively about this project. We wanted to tell our son what a mistake he had made, but we held our tongues and pitched in to help him make the duplex livable. I remember the weekend we spent helping Brad and Jay strip, clean, and paint. But what a change took place over the following week! Bookcases were filled and furniture was arranged; working together, those two young men created a place that was perfectly suited to their needs.

But Brad and Jay had even more creative plans for that property. Within the next two years they were offered twice what they had paid for it—but no sale. Instead, they tore down the building and built two separate three-story units, complete with ocean views, to bring their brides home to. What creative foresight!

From our little family came children who learned creativity at home and then used that creativity to establish their own very different look. They have created their own special retreats to come home to after busy, hardworking days. And one day their children will use their God-given creativity to impart warmth and beauty to their own homes.

Exercising our creativity is one way to be responsible stewards of the gifts and talents God has given us—and to rejoice in our identity as God's children, made in his image. As images of the Creator, we have the opportunity to fashion our lives and our homes into works of art. We can choose to be creative today and every day!

Simple Secrets

❧ Design a "love shelf" in your home to display those little creative gifts from friends and family that mean so much but don't seem to fit anywhere.

❧ Next time you "shop the sales," buy a sheet in colors to match one of your rooms. Use it to cover a pillow or a wall—or make a drape or curtain with it. If you don't sew, wrap or tie it around the pillow or drape it on brass hooks over the window.

☙ Take a class or workshop and learn a new skill that will help you express yourself creatively. Quilting, pottery, creative writing, or even woodworking can be wonderful ways to give your spirit a lift and beautify your environment as well.

☙ Mark off time on your calendar for baking bread, practicing piano, or whatever stimulates your creative juices. Creative time is just like any time; if it's not scheduled, something else will probably crowd it out. Be sure to build in time for dreaming and mistakes. Creativity needs room to flourish.

☙ Use your imagination in displaying your collection of cups and saucers, bells, dolls, thimbles, or salt-and-pepper shakers. A side table, shelf, or armoire serve beautifully, but so might a printer's tray, a special basket, or a windowsill. One friend of mine displayed her collection of teddy bears in a clean but dysfunctional fireplace.

☙ If you don't have a collection, start one. You'll have fun, and your family and friends will never lack for gift-giving ideas. Some more ideas: pitchers, cookie jars, music boxes. One academically minded gentleman we know collects university T-shirts. (He displays his collection on himself!)

☙ During the fall, go out to a local farm and pick pumpkins for centerpieces, yard decorations, and, of course, pumpkin pie! Better yet, plant a package of seeds in July for a fall harvest.

☙ Throw a pretty tablecloth over your coffee table and serve hors d'oeuvres, tea, coffee, or dessert in the living room or den instead of the dining room or kitchen. Or try setting up a card table for dinner in the garden. Your family or your guests will love the change of pace.

☙ Just a little creative touch can make an everyday table extra special. Tie a ribbon around your napkins; add a fresh flower, a few dried flowers, or a piece of ivy.

ॐ Before throwing away something that is worn or broken, consider creative ways to reuse it. A cracked mug or a lovely old teapot with a broken lid can show off a silk flower arrangement. Worn-out jeans cut into strips can be crocheted into a sturdy rug. And almost anything can make a beautiful, interesting wall decoration.

ॐ For an extra-homey dinner, try using a quilt as a tablecloth. Or drape a worn-out sofa with a bright quilt to camouflage and decorate at the same time.

ॐ Take advantage of a free hour to write a story for your children or grandchildren—or some other child in your life. Draw illustrations and send it as a surprise, or read it onto an audiotape for bedtime pleasure.

ॐ At dinner, place individual candles in front of the place settings. Let guests and family members light their own candles and describe something they are thankful for or the best thing that happened that day.

ॐ Collect odd-shaped perfume bottles and display them on a mirrored tray or a high windowsill.

ॐ If you sing or play an instrument, offer to share the gift of your creativity with a local rest home or daycare center. You don't have to be a polished performer to share a lot of joy.

ॐ A plate or basket of fresh fruit on the nightstand adds color and fragrance to the room before it becomes a bedtime snack.

ॐ Small Perrier water bottles make great bud vases. Tie a tiny bow around the neck of the bottle and fill it with flowers. Place in front of each person's plate at dinner, or take one to a friend who needs cheering up.

ॐ Spend a free Saturday stenciling a wall or a floor to add that special "custom" look to any room.

❧ Be creative in finding ways to store sewing or craft supplies. Cover matching boxes to stack in a corner or stow under a bed. Stow your sewing machine on a bookshelf and cover with a fabric "cozy"; other sewing supplies can sit beside it in a pretty basket.

❧ Make creative giving a tradition in your household. In addition to modeling creativity for your kids, provide supplies, space, instruction, and encouragement to make their own cards and gifts—and show how much you treasure their efforts by displaying them prominently.

❧ Above all, think "beauty in the ordinary." A secret of creativity is flowers in a Mason jar.

Chapter 3

In today's world...it is still women's business to make life better, to make tomorrow better than today.

—HELEN THAMES RALEY

The Secret of Femininity

*W*hen I was a little girl, I used to dream of being a "lady." The world of *Little Women,* with its gracious manners and old-fashioned, flowing dresses fascinated me. Softness and lace, tantalizing fragrance and exquisite texture, a nurturing spirit and a love of beauty—these images of femininity shaped my earliest ideas of loveliness.

Is that kind of femininity a lost value today? I don't believe it. The world has changed, and most of us live in simple skirts or business suits or jeans instead of flowing gowns. But I still believe that somewhere in the heart of most of us is a little girl who longs to be a lady.

I also believe that today's world is hungering to be transformed by the spirit of femininity. What better antidote for an impersonal and violent society than warm, gentle, feminine strength? What better cure for urban sprawl and trashed-out countrysides than a love of beauty and a confidence in one's ability to make things lovely? What better hope for the future than a nurturing mother's heart that is more concerned for the next generation than for its own selfish desires? All these qualities—gentle strength, love of beauty, care and nurturing—are part of femininity.

Being a woman created by God is such a privilege—and the gift of our femininity is something we can give both to ourselves and to the people around us. Just one flower, one candle, can warm up a cold, no-nonsense atmosphere with an aura of "I care." Women have always had the ability to transform an environment, to make it comfortable and inviting. I believe we should rejoice in that ability and make the most of it.

This doesn't mean we have to follow a set pattern or adopt a cookie-cutter style. Specific expressions of femininity vary greatly. When I think "feminine," I usually think of soft colors, lace, and flowers. I love ruffled curtains and flower-sprigged wallpaper, delicate bone china and old-fashioned garden prints. And I feel especially beautiful when I'm dressed up in soft and colorful fabrics.

But I know women with vastly different styles who still exude that special quality I call femininity—women who wear tailored tweeds or casual cottons (or gardening "grubbies") with an air of gentleness and sensitivity. Women who fill sleek modern kitchens or utilitarian office cubicles with that unmistakable sense of warmth, caring, and responsiveness. Women who combine self-confidence and an indomitable spirit with a gracious humility and a tender teachability. Women who wear the spirit of femininity with the grace with which they wear their favorite elegant scent.

In recent years we have been obsessed with figuring out what a woman should be allowed to do. God says in his Word a woman can do anything; the point is not what she does but what she is.

—ANNE ORTLUND

To me, the spirit of femininity is expressed in objects chosen for their beauty as well as their usefulness...and lovingly cared for. It is people accepted and nurtured, loveliness embraced and shared. More important, the spirit of femininity is the spirit of care and compassion. In my mind, the most feminine woman is one with an eye and ear for others and a heart for God.

Nurturing the Gift of Femininity

At its best, our femininity arises naturally out of who we are and finds its expression in the way we live our lives and make our homes. But in our hectic, hard-driving society, it's easy to lose track of our gentle, feminine side. Femininity is something we must nurture in ourselves and in our homes, and celebrate as God's gift to us.

Femininity can be cultivated in many ways. A few drops of fragrant oil or perfume in the bathwater. A daisy on your desk. A lace scarf or an embroidered hanky in your pocket. A crocheted shawl around your shoulders. Whatever awakens a calm and gentle spirit within you will nurture beauty in your life.

The expression of femininity is a very personal thing, for it is an expression of a woman's unique self. It is closely tied with identity and with style. Many of the most feminine women I know develop a signature or trademark that marks their distinctiveness. One woman always wears hats. Another enhances her distinctive presence with a favorite fragrance. Still another adopts a theme or motif that becomes part of her identity.

My friend Marilyn's theme is roses. All her correspondence is "rosy," whether with a sticker, a rubber stamp, or her own distinctive stationery. Her home, too, is full of roses—on everything from bedspreads to dessert dishes to rose-scented potpourri.

Marita, one of my publicists, loves rabbits. When she was little, her nickname was "Bunny," and she has carried this trademark into adulthood. Marita and her husband, Chuck, have bunny T-shirts and bunny candle holders, and

at one time even a live bunny as a pet. Anytime I see anything with a rabbit on it I think of Marita, and at Christmas
or on her birthday she always gets a bunny gift. Finding
personalized presents is fun for me and Marita. It's one way
of celebrating her unique, feminine personality.

Rejoicing in the Senses

Femininity includes a wholesome sensuality—a rejoicing
in the fragrances and textures and sounds of God's world.
We honor God and express our own femininity when we
become excited about the beauty around us, when we cultivate the senses that God created in us.

What is the first thing you do when you pick a rose? You
put it to your nose to enjoy the fragrance. How does it
make you feel? Maybe it brings a pleasant memory of that
little girl inside you—of a time when you picked a flower
for your mother or grandmother.

Beautiful fragrances can waft the beauty of femininity all
around the house. A lavender sachet thrown in your under-
wear drawer, sewing box, or stocking box—or hung on a
hanger in the closet—imparts its delicate fragrance at the
most unexpected times. Spray a little cologne on your
notepaper, the bathroom throw rug, or even the toilet
bowl. Fill your house with pine at Christmas, or boil a little
pot of cinnamon and other spices on the stove.

And enjoy your other senses as well. Put on lively music
while you do your housework, and take time out to dance
before the Lord. Experiment with herbs and spices in your
cooking, and don't be afraid to try new dishes. Slipcover a
rough-textured sofa with a cool, smooth sheet, and banish
your scratchy, uncomfortable sweaters.

There is nothing self-indulgent or worldly about such
small pleasures when we approach them with a spirit of
gratitude because God's gifts help us go about the tasks he
has given us. When we feel that the little things in our lives

are pleasant and satisfying, it's amazing how the outside stresses and disappointments fade, at least for the moment. We can then regroup, prioritize, and pray—cultivating a quiet, feminine spirit and preparing ourselves to be God's people in the world.

Surrounded by Beauty

Nurturing femininity in our lives begins with caring for ourselves, with celebrating our unique assets of body and spirit.

Look at your body. How unlike a man's it is! The rest of you is different too—even the structure of your brain. Did you know that women have a higher pain threshold, a keener sense of smell, and better integration between the right and left sides of our brains? I believe we are meant to rejoice in those special feminine qualities that God has gifted us with.

Song of Songs celebrates feminine beauty with wonderful poetry. The woman described there had bouncy, flowing hair (like a flock of goats), sparkling teeth, lips like scarlet ribbons, glowing cheeks, a round and smooth neck, gently swelling breasts, and clothing with the fragrance of Lebanon.

Does that describe me? I hope so. At least, I hope I am taking the trouble to make the best of what God has given me. I may not have time for the 12 months of beauty treatments that transformed a little Jewish girl named Esther into the Queen of Persia. I may never look like a model or a movie star or even my best friend. But I can honor God's gift of femininity by taking care of the unique me he has created.

That's one reason I try to be faithful to my exercise program. My daily walks not only help me keep my figure under control, they restore my energy, lift my spirits, and give me a sense of well-being that makes it easier for me to reach out to others.

That's also why I make the effort to prepare healthful foods for me and my family. Shining hair, healthy nails, fresh skin, strong teeth, stress control—all relate directly to the food I put in my body.

I believe it's important to take that little bit of extra time to pluck and color and brush and cream. A fresh haircut, well-shaped nails, soft lips and hands, pink cheeks, curled eyelashes, pressed and mended clothing—these things help me feel more beautiful, and they tell the world that I care enough to cultivate femininity in my life.

Femininity is also why I make the effort to surround myself with beauty in my home. When I do, I feel more beautiful. I experience the joy of sharing beauty with those closest to me. And I am motivated to reach out to others with gentleness and care.

Surely that beautiful woman in Song of Songs did that. Solomon speaks often of perfume filling the air, of lush wildflowers and morning breezes. Beauty was all around her, from the wildflowers in Sharon to the lily in the mountain valley.

I imagine this woman kept fresh flowers around her home, their fragrances permeating the atmosphere. I imagine she kept the petals and pods from the dried flowers and piled them in a container, adding fragrant oils to make what today we call potpourri. This was sprinkled in her clothing, which perhaps sat stacked neatly in piles. It's hard to say what her life was like then—how her home, rooms, furniture, and cooking area functioned. But I'm sure her home was simple yet beautiful. I'm sure it nurtured the spirit of femininity in her and helped her extend a spirit of caring to others.

One Christmas our daughter, Jenny, gave me a set of three little glass oil lamps—smooth crystal circles with miniature white wicks. I love those oil lamps and light them almost every day. I use them throughout the house, especially in the bath by the tub or over the dishes in the kitchen sink. The glow of those prism lights against the window or ceiling always imparts a sense of peace to my heart. They cast shadows against the walls and send out a rainbow of soft colors that make me feel I'm in the clouds. Somehow I always feel more lovely, more feminine, when those little lamps are glowing.

I remember my feelings the first time I bought a set of ruffled sheets for our bed; I felt caressed and beautiful. My Bob huffed and puffed, claiming that those ruffles almost smothered him. And yet it wasn't long before he admitted that he liked the welcoming softness of our private room. Ten years later, ruffles and eyelet-edged sheets still embellish our bed. I've even taken lace and ruffles off old sheets and sewn them onto new ones. Both he and I appreciate the gentleness that little touch of femininity adds to our lives.

Beauty from the Heart

Yet as much as I believe in taking care of myself and my environment, I know that if I put all my energy into self-care I have missed the whole point. The true beauty of femininity comes from within. If that beauty is lacking, no exercise program, eating plan, wardrobe update, or beauty treatment can put it there. No interior decorating scheme can give it to me. Ruffles and perfume are no substitute for inner beauty.

True femininity comes from the *heart,* and I nurture it when I pay attention to what is really important in life. That's why I need the message of 1 Peter 3:3-5:

> Your beauty should not come from outward
> adornment, such as braided hair and the

wearing of gold jewelry and fine clothes. Instead, it should be that of your inner self, the unfading beauty of a gentle and quiet spirit, which is of great worth in God's sight. For this is the way the holy women of the past who put their hope in God used to make themselves beautiful.

One Christmas our daughter-in-law, Maria, gave me a small pink satin heart with soft lace around it and a pink satin ribbon to hang it by. The scent is soft and gentle. I keep it hung in my bathroom by my makeup area as a reminder not only of her love and thoughtfulness, but also of God's tender, nurturing love to me.

Do you realize that those are "feminine" words for God? Don't be surprised or put off by that. If we women are made in God's image, it only makes sense that we derive our femininity from him. The Bible's word pictures for God are full of soft, tender "feminine" images. God is not only the powerful father; he also displays a tender, nurturing, "motherly" side. We honor God when we rejoice in our femininity and let it transform the world around us.

Femininity is so much more than lace and flowers. A feminine woman is a woman with a teachable heart—a heart that can give and forgive, protect and respect, go from craze to praise. Wrap all that up with a pink satin ribbon (or an earthy, handwoven shawl), and you have the kind of feminine woman that the book of Proverbs says is "worth far more than rubies" (31:10).

The fragrance of that small heart sachet reminds me of the beautiful fragrance of the Lord Jesus himself and that I am called to be a woman after God's own heart. I pray that his love might permeate my heart and the hearts of those around me, that from my life might flow his love and his peace, his spirit and his joy.

That's what I believe we do when we nurture femininity in our lives. We are not just primping and polishing; we are wrapping God's Word around our homes, filling it with prayer, peace, and pleasure. That is the beautiful gift that comes with the spirit of femininity.

Feminine Strength

The spirit of femininity may be gentle and tender, but it is far from weak. Filling our lives with loveliness takes physical stamina, emotional strength, and spiritual courage. And that's no modern, feminist secret. Beautiful women of all ages have shaped the world with the power of their femininity.

I think of Queen Esther standing in the inner court of the palace, resplendent in her royal robes, risking her life to save her people. Or that admirable (if a bit intimidating) woman in Proverbs 31 managing a household and a business while still finding time for volunteer work. Or my own sweet mother, who ran a little dress shop to support us after my father died, and who taught me to love beauty and reach out in love to other people.

Or what about Sarah Edwards, the wife of the famous theologian Jonathan Edwards? In the early 1700s, with no modern conveniences, she watched over a household and raised 11 children. She made all the family's clothes, cooked and prepared all the food, worked the garden, made candles, and stoked the fire. Many guests filled their busy Colonial home. She taught her children to work hard, respect others, and show good manners. And she surrounded all her teaching with her love for God and each child.

All of this time, hard work, and love showed up in the children's accomplishments and attitudes. Her children passed on this same love and discipline to their children. Timothy Dwight, Sarah's grandson and president of Yale

University, said, "All that I am and all I will ever be I owe to my mother."

Strong, beautiful femininity is part of our heritage as women. When we make the effort to cultivate gentle strength, we not only enrich our own lives and make life a little better for those we encounter, we also pass on femininity to the next generation.

Passing the feminine spirit on to our daughters can be done in many ways. We do it when we teach girls the secrets of caring for themselves and others. We do it when we share our pride and skills in such classic "domestic arts" as cooking, sewing, knitting, crocheting, and embroidery.

When I was eight years old, my mother was so ill I had to live with an aunt for a year. Among other things, that wonderfully feminine woman taught me how to arrange flowers, picking them so the stems were long and adding ferns as greenery to the bouquet. In the process she also taught me to glory in my femininity.

But passing on the torch of womanhood is so much more than teaching sewing or flower arranging (and these skills are no prerequisite for femininity). To me, passing on the heritage of femininity is most of all a process of teaching values—caring for ourselves and others, shaping a godly and welcoming atmosphere in our homes and our lives, and working hard to affirm life, making the spirit of loveliness a priority.

The time we spend teaching our daughters—biological and spiritual—about the joys and responsibilities of womanhood will provide benefits for generations to come. And we teach best by what we are, not by what we say.

That's why I pray, "Lord, may the love of Christ permeate my heart and life and spread its gentle fragrance into the lives and hearts of those I meet each day. May the gentle but strong spirit of femininity in my life add beauty and meaning to generations to come."

Simple Secrets

❦ Next time you take a walk, pick a few flowers. Tuck them in a vase by your bed…on your husband's side.

❦ To add a touch of caring and whimsy, use stickers or rubber stamps on your notes and letters—even bills. Write with colored pens, use colored paper clips, and tuck in sprinkles of confetti for a festive message.

❦ Scent your sheets with baby powder or sweet perfume before crawling into bed. You'll enjoy a welcome sense of relaxation—as well as feeling absolutely beautiful.

❦ Hang a tuneful wind chime out on the patio and enjoy its music on breezy evenings.

❦ Collect perfume samples and scented inserts from magazine ads to freshen your drawers or suitcases. Or try spraying your own cologne on the drawer liners to give a scent of you.

❦ Take a hint from great-grandmother: Dab a bit of vanilla behind your ears for a tasty fragrance.

❦ Invest in something pretty to wear while you walk or work out. A colorful leotard, a soft pink set of sweats, or just a bright headband can help you feel beautiful while you work to be beautiful.

❦ String one-inch white eyelet along the edge of your closet shelf. Attach it with thumbtacks, a hot glue gun, or a heavy-duty stapler for a great feminine look.

❦ Use spray adhesive, staples, or a hot glue gun to cover shoeboxes with floral wrapping paper or wallpaper for your shoes. They look great on the floor or shelf.

❦ Pick up a set of inexpensive black or cobalt blue dishes if you see them on sale. Food looks especially beautiful against a dark background.

ঌ If you wear a suit to the office, try the old-fashioned custom of wearing a rosebud or a tiny bunch of violets on your lapel. Ask your local florist about tiny holders that can keep your flowers fresh.

ঌ Enjoy a bubble bath by candlelight while sipping iced tea or warm cocoa.

ঌ Take an afternoon off to play "dress up" with a little girl in your life. Deck yourselves out in your finery, help her put on a little makeup and jewelry, and visit a local tea room for ice cream or a muffin.

ঌ If you work at home, consider your everyday "look"—is it casual or just sloppy? Why not get up ten minutes early to fix yourself for the people you love most?

ঌ Get inspired by reading the story of a great woman of the past or present. Some ideas: Margaret of Cortona, Elizabeth Fry, Dolly Madison, Lottie Moon, Amy Carmichael, Elisabeth Elliot, Ruth Bell Graham, Mother Teresa.

ঌ Make a pretty cover for your Bible or notebook out of fabric or paper. Tape the words to 1 Peter 3:3-5 inside as a reminder to cultivate your inner beauty.

ঌ Invest in some classical tapes or CDs to give your home a touch of culture. As a start, try a collection of Strauss waltzes, Handel's *Water Music*, Mozart's sonatas, or Schumann's *Kinderlieder*.

ঌ In the spring, take a child (or yourself) for a "senses walk." Smell the roses, the orange blossoms, the sweet peas; see how many different fragrances you can detect. Gently pull the stamen from a honeysuckle blossom and taste the nectar. Close your eyes and listen for different sounds—a bird, train, foghorn, airplane, saw, hammer. Look around and try to count how many colors you can detect.

ঌ Do you remember finding a smooth stone and loving its cool touch? Find another one. As you hold it in your hand, thank God for the strong and lovely gift of your femininity.

Chapter 4

Don't let artificial light and city streets keep you from noticing sunsets and sunrises, from experiencing the spring of new life and the harvest of fall. If you don't have a farm, at least have a window box or a few pots of earth.

—M. Basil Pennington
A Place Apart

The Secret of the Garden

*A*ccording to the Bible, we human beings started out in a garden. Maybe that's why green, growing things do so much for us. Gardens are places of life, growth, rebirth. Working with plants and soil is a therapeutic experience to our stressed-out lives.

You don't have to have acres of land or an emerald thumb in order for gardening to be part of your life. Your garden can flourish in whatever space and time you have to give it.

In our first apartment, Bob and I barely had room for ourselves, let alone space for a garden plot. But I was able to unleash the spirit of the garden even in that tiny place by setting out some small pots of geraniums in a kitchen window that received early-morning sun. Before long, blooms had brightened our little home. Soon after, I added pots of herbs on that kitchen shelf. Bob was amazed that I could season our meals with a pinch or two of herbs from my window garden.

That was just the start of our apartment garden. When I went to the market, I would occasionally pick up a potted plant in a gallon container. Those little "instant gardens" would travel around the apartment, ending up at the middle of the breakfast table while we ate, on the bathroom vanity while I took a bubble bath, or on the nightstand while we flipped through magazines and dreamed of the beautiful landscaped grounds we would love to have someday.

When we lived in the Barnes Barn, Bob and I had plenty of room for that magazine garden we wanted so many years ago. Our home was on garden tours in our city. We loved to hear people respond, "How beautiful it is!" "How can you ever leave it to travel?" "What a relaxing retreat center!" and especially "I would love to live here!"

We also heard, "Why go to all that trouble to keep it up?"

For me, the answer to that question goes back to those early years when God was preparing my heart to appreciate his beauty through our garden. At that point I just knew I wanted a flower in a vase by my bed or in the center of our dining room table. Over the years, God used that simple desire to get me outside.

For Bob, who comes from a three-generation farm family, the spirit of the garden goes back even further. Bob truly has a green thumb. It seems that everything he plants grows. He is the one primarily responsible for helping our garden flourish so beautifully around our home.

But Bob and I both love being involved with growing things. Even the hard work—weeding, checking for insects, watering—feels purposeful and worthwhile. And then what joy to see a blanket of green outside our door or the bright splashes of color on our patio! What a thrill to pick that first plum, orange, avocado, bean, corn, zinnia, marigold, or squash in our spring and summer gardens! We are so much richer because of our love for plants, flowers, and trees and our involvement in their growth.

Something Out of Nothing

Let me encourage you to find room for a garden in your life, for a garden has secrets that can teach you so much. In it we have the privilege of witnessing firsthand a part of God's character: creation.

Genesis 1:1-2 tells us that "in the beginning...the earth was formless and void" (NASB). From that bleak beginning God began the process of creation. From "formless and void" sprang forth light and color; oceans and skies; lots and lots of green, growing things; animals; and finally people. Out of nothing, God created the whole earth in all its beauty and complexity.

"Formless and void," or maybe *"farmless* and void," describes the lot around the first home Bob and I were able to purchase. It was a tract home in a new area, and the small square lot was truly void (except for a few weeds in the corner of the backyard).

But not for long! With information and ideas gained from observing other homes, poring through regional magazines, and visiting our local nurseries, we started filling the "farmless void" of our new home. We designed and installed our sprinkler system. (That was before automatic and drip systems.) We selected our trees in five-gallon containers. We rototilled the soil, scattered lawn seed, and topped it all with fertilizer. Then we sat back and waited for nature to fill our void with "farm."

Oh, how I wish it had been that easy. It seemed that the weeds came up first and were bigger than the shrubs! But that first home was a great learning laboratory—Basic Gardening 101. We learned some valuable lessons, such as:

1. Some plants do better in the shade than in the sun.

2. Not all plants grow well in our region.

3. When planting trees, the hole needs to be twice as big as the ball of the tree, and we need to spend as much on the planting mix as we did for the tree.

4. Weeds need to be pulled as soon as they are big enough to pull—not after they have spread all over the yard.

5. A good, balanced fertilizer needs to be applied on a regular basis.

6. A well-thought-out watering schedule (not too much and not too little) is important for good growth.

7. With a garden, God always gives you a second chance. With time, patience, and fertilizer, even major mistakes can be corrected and beauty will be the result.

But we learned something else, too, as we worked with God to bring "farm" out of the void. We learned some things about the purpose of gardens—and people.

"Out of the ground," the book of Genesis tells us, "the Lord God caused to grow every tree that is pleasing to the sight and good for food....Then the Lord God took the man and put him into the garden of Eden to cultivate it and keep it" (2:9,15 nasb).

What do those verses mean? First, that plants were to serve a double function—to please the eye and to feed the stomach. Second, that human beings were put into the garden to take care of its contents.

In other words, our capacity to enjoy green things and our responsibility as caretakers on the garden of earth are built into our very nature. Doesn't it follow that we are happiest and most productive when we allow that part of our nature to have expression in our lives?

In today's urban society it may not be practical for most of us to grow our own food or take care of a full-blown garden. But there are a million other ways we can cultivate a garden in our homes. Perhaps the simplest way to enjoy gardening is to make liberal use of houseplants. Studies show that plants not only please the eye and soothe the spirit, but they also clean the air of impurities. Windows and porches are obvious and ideal places for sunloving begonias and geraniums. But almost any corner can benefit from a blossom or a touch of green.

Look around you. Where can you use flowers and plants to decorate your home? A brass pot of zinnias on the coffee table that echoes the print in your curtains will do wonders in your living room. And the dark corner of your family room will come alive when you brighten it with a handsome container of philodendron.

Do you have an entry hall? That would be a perfect spot for a bowl of geraniums or chrysanthemums, or a vase of freshly picked roses, to welcome your guests and your family. How about the fireplace in the summertime? A decorative pleated paper fan spread across the empty andirons makes an admirable background for potted jade plants or English ivy.

In any room, a pot of blooming narcissus, hyacinths, or tulips can welcome spring early. Take advantage of "grow your own" kits so you can enjoy the growing too.

If you take a little time to learn how to grow (or buy) and handle flowers, greens, potted plants, shrubs, and vines so that they take their place in home decorating, you will discover that you are not only saving money but beautifying your home as well.

There are even more ambitious ways, of course, to let a garden bring joy to your life. A vegetable plot in the backyard or a flower bed in the front can be a rewarding hobby; we love having both. But gardening need not take up that much time or space. Even a foot-square plot by the porch planted in tulips or peppers can yield a surprising harvest. A single tomato plant in a tub on the patio can keep you in fresh tomatoes all summer.

If you use your creativity, you may be able to think of many other possibilities. An elderly neighbor may be thrilled to swap gardening space in return for help with planting and weeding. Many urban centers have set aside communal garden space where families or individuals can have small plots. Churches, too, have worked together with their poorer neighbors to grow much-needed vegetables.

I've even heard of a group of graduate students living in "married student housing" at a university who obtained permission to plant gardens on the grounds. Many of these were international students homesick for their native cuisine. They took advantage of their little plots to grow vegetables they couldn't find in local markets. But as men and women from many different backgrounds worked the soil together, they quickly learned that a garden allows gardeners to cross boundaries of race and culture.

A Heritage of Gardening

A garden can help people cross generational boundaries as well. Our grandchildren love to be a part of our garden. The whole process is like a living botany laboratory. And the time we spend together working with soil and plants is a perfect opportunity to act out one of our favorite verses of Scripture:

> These words, which I am commanding you today, shall be on your heart. You shall teach them diligently to your sons and shall talk of them when you sit in your house and when you walk by the way and when you lie down and when you rise up (Deuteronomy 6:6-7 NASB).

We use every opportunity to teach our grandchildren about God and creation. Their little hands help till the ground, scatter the seeds in the trenches, cover the seeds with fertile soil, and help with the first watering. We find that children are perfect for these chores—what child doesn't love to dig in the dirt?

Each time they visit (which is often, because they live just five minutes away), they can't get out of the van fast enough to see how the plants are growing. And they can hardly wait for the first harvest. Because there is always more than we need, they get to take some home for their families and also to share with a neighbor.

They share the chores too—weeding, watering, picking snails. Bob often gives them one or more "I Was Caught Being Good" stickers to show his appreciation for their help. He's even been known to take them for a special treat at the local yogurt shop or hamburger stand. Our grandchildren have truly bonded with their "PaPa" by working with him in the yard and the garden.

How Does Your Garden Grow?

As we have worked in the garden over the years, we have garnered bits of wisdom I want to pass along. Attention to the following secrets will help make gardening a pleasant experience. And please note: These techniques can apply on a tiny or a large scale. Even if your garden is a big pot on the back patio

> *The kiss of the sun for pardon, the song of the birds for mirth, one is nearer God's heart in a garden than anywhere else on earth.*
>
> —Dorothy Frances Gurney

with a tomato plant and a marigold or two, you can increase your yields and your pleasure if you consider these elements.

Planning. The difference between a good garden and a great garden often lies in the planning. Although there are no hard and fast rules for planning a garden, a few basic principles will steer you toward success.

First, plan your garden to fit your needs. Do you expect to feed your family from your garden, to enjoy a neighborhood showplace, or just to add a lift to a bleak corner? Do you have long hours to putter in the dirt, or do you need low-maintenance vegetation? How much time (and help) is available to weed, water, plant, repot, or harvest?

Obviously, planning should take into consideration the land you have available. Consider sunlight, drainage, slope, wind, and size and then choose plants that are suited for your area. If you live in northern Minnesota and want to raise avocados, you are probably setting yourself up for frustration.

Above all, in planning, use your imagination! Your garden should be a place where your personality and creative instincts can merge with nature's own designs. Express yourself and rejoice in the privilege of sharing in God's gift of growth.

Preparation. Soil is so much more than just plain dirt. It is a mixture of mineral particles, living organisms, organic matter, air, and water—and it is the foundation not only of your garden, but of all plant life on earth.

In general, soil began as rock. In a weathering process that began long ago and continues today, rock from the earth's crust is slowly broken down into small particles through the action of frost, temperature changes, wind, water, and acids produced by decaying organic matter. Living organisms from microscopic bacteria to earthworms, along with the remains of plants and animals in various stages of decomposition, combine with mineral particles to form a complex, constantly changing system that provides plants with the water, air, and nutrients they need.

What does this mean to us as gardeners? Simply that it pays to spend time preparing the soil. Given the origins of soil, it should come as no surprise that adding organic matter to your garden always improves it. This is the key to soil preparation.

One of the most effective ways to enrich soil is the use of a compost heap. We recycle all of our lawn clippings, leaves, and vegetable food scraps to make a rich humus additive for our garden and shrubs. (In the process, we reduce strain on our local landfill as well.) In the last fifteen years, many commercial compost makers have appeared on the market. Your local nursery or a good book on organic gardening can give you more information on this subject.

The best way to get to know your soil is by working with it, digging through it, examining it, testing it, and improving it. Don't be afraid to get down on your hands and knees and muck around in the dirt. The child in you will be delighted, your fingernails *will* come clean, and your reward will arrive in terms of green, growing loveliness.

Planting. After waiting through winter (and each region has its own particular calendar) and then patiently preparing the garden soil for the upcoming season of growth, it's a special day when planting time finally arrives. In Southern California we are blessed with a long growing season, but each region has its own particular advantages and limitations.

I suggest that you purchase a good regional book (see your nursery owner) or find a good local magazine to help you with your planting. Such a publication will show you not only the "when" but the "what" for your areas and thus increase your chances for success.

Even if you're getting a jump on the season by starting some of your own transplants indoors before outdoor planting is possible, planting seeds can be a very quick process. But indoors or out, it pays to work deliberately and do the job right. I like to mix small seeds with sand or cornmeal and then spread them in the soil. I find that the additives make handling small seeds easier and also give better coverage.

Care. None of us wants to spend all our free time maintaining a garden. But we don't have to. Pulling weeds and cultivating the soil can be done in a few minutes if you understand weeds and anticipate their arrival—pulling the weeds as soon as they can be distinguished from the baby plants. The process can be even less time-consuming if you use an appropriate mulch—a two- to four-inch layer of shredded wood, pine bark chips, grass clippings, or other porous material. Bob has often commented how many fewer weeds we have since he has learned to make his own mulch from grass clippings and chipped wood and spread it around our plants.

If you've planned your garden well—its size, especially—caring for it can be a brief and pleasurable routine. A few minutes a day spent inspecting (and admiring) your plants for signs of insect or disease problems, loosening hard-packed soil, or hoeing away small weeds is all it takes.

Watering will take a bit longer because most vegetables and fruits require slow, deep soakings for best results. Hand watering or using a soaker hose (the flat kind with lots of holes) is better than using a sprinkler.

Don't forget to deep-water those young trees at least once a month during the growing season. Long, slow watering will coax the roots to go down deep and give strength to the tree when high winds blow.

Because we have a lot of ground cover, we continually have to be aware of snails. One snail can devastate a beautiful flower pot or a section of garden. We find that hand picking—going out in the early morning to inspect for snails and then collecting them in a bucket—is the best way to minimize damage.

Harvesting. Your first harvest, a month or so after outdoor planting begins, will probably be small—a handful of lettuce leaves for the first straight-from-the-garden salad, or a few scallions and radishes. But then, as more of the garden matures, the harvest will grow...and grow. In fact, one of the great joys of gardening is seeing, smelling, and touching the bountiful results of this joint effort between you and God.

Our most memorable harvest was the year we planted our first pumpkins. Not ever having planted pumpkins before, we didn't know what to expect. Well, we planted abundantly and we harvested abundantly. We had vines all over the yard, covered with pretty golden-yellow blossoms. At Halloween time we had 69 round, gorgeous, orange pumpkins.

Were we a hit in our neighborhood! No one had to go to the market for pumpkins—they just had to come to PaPa Bob's garden to get the raw materials for scary jack-o'-lanterns and savory pies. We have never grown that many pumpkins again, but we still remember the sheer joy of that harvest.

In midseason, as the early crops mature and the first of the warm-season vegetables (like beans) are ready, you'll be so busy you may forget the thrill of your first haul. Now, whichever direction you turn, there seems to be something that needs picking or processing right away. Finally, at the end of the season, you can harvest and freeze or can for out-of-season eating. There's nothing like a fresh summer vegetable when it's cold outside.

Whenever you do it, harvesting is an exciting and rewarding process. Make a party out of your first picking. And don't forget to share! Now is the time to invite your friends in to pick their own—or take your excess to a local food bank.

One of my richest harvests was when Bob planted a row of sweet peas for me on Valentine's Day. After picking bouquet after bouquet of these fragrant flowers in mid-summer, I told Bob that those sweet peas were the best gift he had ever given me. They furnished a summerlong reminder of Bob's thoughtful love.

Gardening provides so many occasions for sharing and gift-giving! One year, for Bob's birthday, our dear friend Florence mailed him a birthday card with a package of giant sunflower seeds. What wholesome pleasure that simple, practical gift has brought us. We read the directions on the flower package, located a spot in the garden that would provide full sun, and planted the packet of seeds. For years we had a beautiful row of huge, bright-yellow flowers. After the flower petals faded, we dried the seeds in the oven and had a nutritious snack for ourselves, our grandchildren, and the area birds. And yes, we saved enough seeds for next year's planting. Florence's gift of a garden was a gift that kept on giving.

A Deeper Harvest

Gardening yields so much in our lives. It lets us partic-ipate in God's process of creation. It provides wonderful opportunities for teaching and sharing and giving. But I have found that being part of a garden yields a deeper har-vest as well.

Over the years, gardening has taught me a lot about who I am as a woman of God. Through many hours of working alone and with others—tilling, planting, mulching, weeding, pruning, repotting—I have learned to "slow down and smell the roses." I have moved closer to a healthy balance between "doing" and "being." That's because the garden forces me to go at God's pace, taking time from a busy schedule of writing, traveling, and speaking to do the simple daily chores that lead to beauty. It's an eternal rhythm: Sometimes I work, sometimes I wait...then God does the growing and I enjoy the results. I thank God regularly for his gift of the garden.

Wouldn't you love to have visited the first garden God created? It must have been beautiful—fragrant, fruitful, lushly green, yet ordered and balanced. I trust that my life can somehow reflect that same beauty. Yours can too. If your life is "farmless" because you have become convinced that you have a "black thumb," you can still fill up that void with something green or something blooming.

You don't have to turn your home into a greenhouse. Just pay a visit to a nursery or the grocery store or a florist—or visit a neighbor whose thumb is green. Pick a plant or a flower that makes you feel good, and put the pot or vase on your table or nightstand. If necessary, get instructions for the care and feeding of your new plant friend—and follow them. Then stand back and wait for the joy of the garden to begin transforming your life.

Simple Secrets

❧ Fresh flowers have a way of sweetening the air. Try to keep them around. And try lighting a candle near the vase. The combination of flowers and candlelight is a simple but lovely way to make your home beautiful.

❧ There are times when you want a bright floral arrangement in your home, but you don't have the extra money to buy it. Why not learn how to make the arrangement yourself? Look in your local community college catalog for classes, or find a good instruction book.

❧ Think of flowers when you think of the special days in your life that you love to celebrate—births, Easter, Christmas, fall, spring, weddings, christenings. All these moments you treasure are appropriate for a flower or plant.

- For an investment in the future, plant a tree! If you don't have a yard, think about making a "green" donation to your church grounds or even a local school.

- In a kitchen, where so many hours are spent, one spray of fragrant lilac blossoms in a child's battered mug can brighten the day.

- Your front door can always say "welcome" with a May basket, a fall arrangement of Indian corn, or a green wreath for Christmas.

- Try using plants as architectural helps—a group of tall plants to divide a room, for instance, or a combination of potted and hanging plants to partially screen a window.

- If the green or yellow or bittersweet pots you find in a garden shop don't match your pale pink (or bright red) window, just buy white plastic pots and a can of spray paint. In just a few minutes you can have pots to fit your decor.

- Place a row of herb plants you can grow from seed or buy in three-inch pots on the kitchen window. Besides being decorative, they will add distinct flavor to gourmet dishes.

- On the sun porch, fill an attractive wheeled cart with blooming begonias.

- Brighten the dining room with an indoor window box of impatiens.

- Are you on a seed catalog list? Send for every catalog you read about. It's an easy way to learn the names of flowers and a great opportunity to see them in color. And browsing through beautiful catalogs can color a dreary winter day with hopeful brightness.

॒ If time or space prohibit a full garden, plant tomatoes and strawberries in a barrel or other large container. You'll be surprised at the yield from just a few plants.

॒ Order ladybugs from a gardening catalog or nursery and let children help release them around garden or yard. Ladybugs are God's way of keeping harmful bugs under control—and kids love to help them "fly away home."

॒ Try companion planting. Some flowers, such as marigolds, act as natural insect repellents to protect your crops.

॒ Did you ever grow a sweet potato garden as a child? Get a quart-sized jar and a sweet potato, and try it again. (All you have to do is stick the potato in water and wait.) Better yet, share the fun of growing a potato with your favorite child.

॒ For a low-maintenance, high-pleasure garden, scatter a packet of wildflower seeds. If you wait until the seed heads are ripe in the summer before mowing the garden down, it will reseed itself year after year.

Chapter 5

*I am beginning to see that the
things that really matter take
place not in the board rooms, but
in the kitchens of the world.*

—GARY SLEDGE

The Secret of the Kitchen

"No matter where I serve my guests, it seems they like my kitchen best."

That little painted plaque in my kitchen is more than just a cute saying for the wall. It's the way I've felt all my life. Wherever I've lived, the kitchen has always seemed to be the place where warmth and love reign. Family and friends are drawn there like chickens to their roosts. Of all the rooms in our home, the kitchen is the place of comfort, the preferred gathering place for shared conversations and the teamwork of preparing good meals for and with each other.

Much of my young childhood was spent in kitchens. My father was raised as an orphan in the kitchen of a palace in Vienna. He later came to America as a Viennese chef and opened many fine restaurants. In the early 1940s he worked for Fox Studios in Hollywood and created beautiful buffet tables with lavish foods and ice carvings. Many of the old-time movie stars—Clark Gable, Lana Turner, Mario Lanza, and Betty Grable, to name a few—joined in the standing ovations awarded my father for his culinary creations.

For me as a young girl, the kitchen was always where I wanted to be—sitting on the countertop as ingredients flew everywhere, tantalizing aromas floated through the air, and meals and memories were created. Despite the dysfunction of alcoholism that marred those early years, the kitchen was still a wondrous place to me.

Later, after my father died and my mother and I took up quarters in three rooms behind her little dress shop, the kitchen was still the center of warmth. I remember so many times when Mama welcomed me home with a baked potato, hot cocoa, cinnamon apples, or popovers in winter; Popsicles or ice cold lemonade in summer. All these were expressions of love, and they all came from the kitchen.

The Heart of the Home

Even today, the kitchen feels like the heart of home to me. The smell of garlic and onions being sauteed in butter draws me to the kitchen. Coffee, brewing fresh in the pot, lifts and warms my heart. I love to bend over a bubbling pot of soup or gaze out the window while quietly bringing order to my countertops. And I love to smile at all the photographs of family and friends that smile back at me from the refrigerator door.

My kitchen is filled with heart. My pots hang on hooks above the stove the way my dad's pots did in his commercial kitchens. Plants line the windowsill, including a few pots of herbs to snip when needed. A crock holds my whips, wooden spoons, and spatulas in a space-saving and attractive bouquet. A collection of special plaques and pictures from friends and family decorates my "love wall" at one end of the room. The kitchen phone has a long cord so I can catch up on phone calls while I clean my greens and fruit, load the dishwasher, clean a shelf in the refrigerator, start a pot of coffee, or ready a casserole for the oven.

Our current kitchen is spacious and convenient, with lots of pantry and cupboard space. But I have learned that even the smallest of kitchens can be organized, efficient, and inviting.

When our two children, Brad and Jenny, were in high school, we lived in a small condominium with a galley kitchen—and yet those were two of the best kitchen years of our lives. One evening during that time we served Mexican Mountains (tostadas) to 50 football players and ten cheerleaders. Jenny and Brad still remember the fun of chopping tomatoes, grating cheese, mashing avocados, and slicing olives for that get-together, and their friends reminisce about the fun of crowding into that little condo (and overflowing into the garage) for an evening of fun.

To make better use of your cooking space, take a little time to streamline your kitchen down to just the things you really use. Most of today's cooking is simple and fast, and many dishes can be brought right to the table and attractively served in the cooking pot. So eliminate the outdated stuff you don't like or use. And make a list of new items you would like to try; kitchen "wishes" make great birthday and Christmas gifts.

Above all, make your kitchen a room you enjoy and feel good in. A fresh paint job, new knobs on the doors, or just a thorough cleaning and rearranging will do wonders. What about a radio on the shelf? And don't forget a kitchen stool to save your back and legs while preparing a salad or vegetable—and maybe a stepstool to help you reach those high shelves.

If your counter space is limited, you can make more space by keeping the toaster, coffeepot, and other equipment or appliances in the cupboards, yet within easy reach. Sometimes, when I need more prep space, I'll put my breadboard on top of my electric stovetop and use it to grate or chop.

Baskets are great to hang in the kitchen or across hearths in a country dining room. They always warm up the feel of the kitchen, and they serve double duty as serving containers. I use my baskets often for countless purposes. The smaller ones hold chips or rolls. A flat, shallow basket, lined with foil and fluffy lettuce leaves, becomes a raw veggie platter with a scooped-out red cabbage to hold the dip. (Seeded red and green bell peppers also make colorful dip bowls.) A casserole looks especially warm and inviting nestled in an appropriate-size basket.

Making the Most of Mealtime

Much of our lifetime is spent in a food-related atmosphere. If you are a woman 45 years or older, you've already spent over 50,000 hours in the kitchen and eaten more than 50,000 meals! Since we spend so much of our lives eating, preparing to eat, and cleaning up after eating, shouldn't we put some effort and attention into making mealtimes some of the most pleasurable and memorable parts of our lives?

What makes a memorable meal? The recipe for such a time involves four simple ingredients:

The Setting. The attractive way you set the table sets the tone for a meal and can convey affection, warmth, and caring. The simple way the napkin is fluffed up in the glass, folded to make a flower, or creatively arranged in a napkin ring can speak your love and concern. A garnish of parsley on a platter of roast chicken or a wedge of lemon in a glass of water say, "I care enough to do the little bit it takes to be above average." A floral sheet made into a unique tablecloth with matching napkins can be creative and inexpensive.

Centerpieces are great for establishing a mood. But a centerpiece can be so much more than a vase of chrysanthemums plopped in the middle of a table. An autumn table lined down the middle with apples, pears, grapes, winter squash, and Indian corn smiles a beautiful welcome.

A swatch of pine twinkling with tiny white lights and festive with tiny wooden toys sets a Christmasy mood. Individual vases holding single blooms can freshen up individual place settings. And candles are always wonderful. Use them liberally to create the spirit of warmth at mealtime.

The Food. Obviously, food takes the starring role at any meal. The warm, caring spirit of the kitchen extends to providing food that is both delicious and healthful. The old adage, "You are what you eat," really is true. When we eat right, we look better and feel better. Our mental and physical health improves. We have more energy and endurance to carry out the task of loving others.

Given the fact that healthy eating is so important, isn't it great that healthy meals can also taste wonderful? Many of the most healthy foods—fruits and vegetables, especially—are also the most pleasing to the eye. Learning to eat a wholesome variety of foods can be a delicious adventure that adds another exciting dimension to the beauty of your kitchen.

When you are planning your meals, doing your shopping, or just puttering in the kitchen, don't forget to take your nose into account! Aromas are memory triggers; they invoke recollections of past happiness. You can build those kinds of memories through the wonderful aromas of the kitchen. The smell of garlic, curry, cinnamon, fresh bread, or coffee can combine with wonderful tastes and warm feelings to instill lovely

> *Eating is the ritual of communion; over a lifetime, it gives us opportunities for a continual flow of creativity, and for unique personal expression—a chance to delight and nourish the spirit as well as strengthen the body.*
>
> —ALEXANDRIA STODDARD

memories of the gifts of the kitchen deep in the souls of your family, your guests, and you.

The Fellowship. Mealtime is traditionally a time for family and guests to gather and share their lives. But hectic schedules have made family meals a thing of the past for many people. It's worth the effort to buck this trend at least once in awhile and share a family meal. Turn off the TV, unplug the phone, and sit down together for a time of fellowship and food.

Expect some resistance if your family is out of practice at fellowship. You might want to stimulate conversation with some questions such as "What is the best thing that happened to you today?" Be prepared to share, and be prepared to listen.

Mealtime is not the only opportunity for "kitchen style" fellowship, of course. Some of my most treasured conversations have happened while two of us were cooking or cleaning up together. After-school snacks, afternoon tea, and late-night popcorn sessions all provide safe, comfortable opportunities for sharing lives.

Some of the richest kind of kitchen fellowship comes when we extend the blessings of the kitchen to those outside our homes and families. Surely this is part of what Jesus meant when he said, "I was hungry and you fed me." People who volunteer to cook at a soup kitchen, deliver meals on wheels, or help with an emergency food drive discover that they are richly blessed by the opportunity to share their lives with someone in need.

A Peaceful Ambience. "Better a dry crust with peace and quiet than a house full of feasting with strife" (Proverbs 17:1). That was true in Solomon's day, and it's especially true in today's high-stress, stomach-churning society. Peaceful mealtimes aid both the digestion and the disposition; they are well worth the effort they take.

How can mealtimes be more relaxed? Careful planning helps so that dishes are ready at the same time and you don't have to keep running to the kitchen. Food should be simple and wholesome and tailored to the needs of family and guests. (Serving spicy or difficult-to-handle food to small children, for example, just invites tension and frustration.) Conversation can be lively and even provocative, but it's good to postpone weighty or emotional issues for another time. Beautiful, soothing music in the background helps everyone to calm down and enjoy the meal.

Perhaps the most meaningful and effective way to bring an air of peace and grace to mealtime is to make a habit of inviting God to be present. Even a mumbled and hurried "Bless this food to the nourishment of our bodies" can help turn our hearts in the direction of gratitude and peace. But how much better to really stop, hold hands, and ask the Lord's blessing on the meal and those gathered around the table.

The Year-Round Kitchen

I find that my cooking-and-kitchen decor changes with the seasons. And I enjoy the gentle rhythm of such seasonal change.

In summer, I display all my fresh fruit and vegetables in a wooden bowl or basket. In fall, I love having pumpkins, squash, and gourds in a bowl or on a countertop. Flowers in my spring window will be asters and daffodils. Summer is daisies, sweet peas, pansies, and sweet-smelling roses. Fall brings brilliant chrysanthemums, and winter a potted fern or geranium.

The foods I serve vary with the seasons as well. Certain foods should be eaten at certain times of the year. I find this to be true even in Southern California, where the growing season is long and the variety of available produce is incredible. What is worse than a tasteless hothouse tomato in the winter or a mushy, tasteless apple in July? The best way to select fresh ingredients is to shop in season, if at all possible.

Strawberries and asparagus, for example, are delectable in the spring. It is during this season that I love to serve fresh meals on a white lace tablecloth. As the first fruits of the harvest begin to make their appearance—tiny new potatoes, delicate lettuce—I enjoy serving meals that celebrate their arrival. And what a time for flowers! I love a spring table blooming with the first flowers of spring.

Summer brings barbecues, campouts, and cookouts—along with wonderful melons, sweet corn, and crisp cucumbers. It's a time for being outdoors and enjoying the longer days. We love to wrap our fresh, buttered corn-on-the-cob in foil and put it on the outdoor grill with chicken marinated in lemon juice, butter or oil, and spices. I also wrap zucchini and yellow crookneck squash in foil and put it on the barbecue. A big green salad with lots of sliced assorted vegetables, tossed with a garlic dressing, is enough to make me pray for a long, hot summer!

I love shopping at fruit-and-vegetable stands in the spring and summer. In addition, farmer's markets are becoming more popular and accessible sources of home-grown goodies. Many times farm families sell home-baked breads, honey, nuts, and jam as well. In the face of such abundance, I always feel like a kid in a candy store.

Fall brings the excitement of harvest and the golden colors and heartier flavors of pumpkins, squash, apples, and pears. As the holiday season draws nearer, the kitchen becomes fragrant with holiday baking—the traditional breads, cakes, pies, cookies, and turkey with the works. (But I make turkey almost year-round too. It's easy and delicious, and we all enjoy the leftover turkey for sandwiches, salads, and crepes.) As the weather grows cooler, my kitchen warms with soups, Crock-Pot meals, and casseroles.

The seasonal parade of foods will vary widely according to where you live, but tuning in to the turning of the seasons will help make your kitchen more warming and fulfilling.

Whatever the season, it takes so little to make room for the warm comfort of the kitchen in our everyday lives. Setting a pretty breakfast table or food bar with placemats sends out good signals. Putting a chicken in the Crock-Pot before leaving for work takes less than ten minutes and yields warm, fragrant dividends at the end of the day. Sharing secrets and concerns over tea, dinner, or the dishes helps us draw closer in love to one another. If you take the time to be in the kitchen, every cupboard and every countertop can transform your life and your home with delicious warmth and beauty.

Simple Secrets

- Make your kitchen a place that says "Welcome." A bowl of freshly washed lemons is a great way to say "Hello!"

- Make the inside of your refrigerator a feast for the eye. Use see-through containers for fruit. A bouquet of parsley in a small glass adds a fresh touch. Even a small bowl of flowers can bless the eye of anyone looking for a snack.

- After baking an apple pie, set it on the counter to cool—and perfume the house. Try piling some fresh apples next to it for a delightful "before and after" look.

- Serve your butter in a white pottery crock. Whip it with an equal amount of olive oil to reduce calories and stretch the butter. It will fluff up beautifully.

❧ Freeze grapes and roll them in granulated sugar. Store in a glass bowl or on a pretty plate and toss in a salad or use as a garnish.

❧ For a creative surprise, serve breakfast for dinner. Our family loves waffles with toppings of fruit, nuts, coconut, raisins, jam, maple syrup, and yogurt.

❧ Store foods in ways that allow them to be decorative as well as useful. Display fruit in a basket or special bowl on the kitchen table or drainboard. Stack potatoes and onions in a basket and use it to enliven an out-of-the way corner of your counter or floor.

❧ Break the iceberg lettuce habit when it comes to salad. Combine spinach, leaf lettuce, romaine, or red-tip lettuce together with bean sprouts, mushrooms, red onion rings, and your favorite dressing for a fresher, healthier salad. Or try adding red cabbage and a sprinkle of goat cheese or freshly grated Parmesan.

❧ Garlic adds great flavor to many dishes and is very healthful. Add it to soups, chicken, roasts, and Crock-Pot meals. Try hanging fresh garlic on a rope in your kitchen—and use it.

❧ Popovers and other quick breads let you put fresh bread on the table in a hurry. Or stir up a batch of blueberry or cranberry muffins for a sweet and colorful bread treat.

❧ Next time you make buttered toast, sprinkle on some cinnamon and sugar. An old idea, but when was the last time you did it?

❧ Put your olive oil and wine vinegar in pretty decanters by your stove. I like to make a seasoned olive oil by combining two dried red peppers (the long, thin kind), the seeds from two more red peppers, one tablespoon each of rosemary and thyme, and four cloves of garlic in a quart jar and covering with olive oil. Or just put a few cloves of garlic in a glass bottle and fill with oil.

❧ Add one-half teaspoon ground cinnamon and a pinch of ground cloves to your coffee grounds next time you brew. Drink out of your favorite cup and saucer and enjoy the fresh flavor and smell.

❧ Use a pepper mill and grind your own pepper fresh at the table.

❧ On a slow afternoon, put on soft music and browse through your favorite recipe book for ideas and inspiration.

❧ Set aside a Saturday morning to learn how to use one of those appliances stored away in a low cabinet. Are you secretly afraid of your pressure cooker? Have you never cooked anything but frozen dinners in your microwave? Has your food processor gathered dust since you bought it? Take the time to find out what these helpers can do—and then decide whether you really require their services. You may be surprised by what goes and what stays.

❧ Hang a basket or two—or thirty!—from the ceiling beam or over a wall in the kitchen or breakfast room.

❧ "Dejunk" your kitchen 15 minutes at a time. The room will look more spacious, and you'll be more inspired to spend time there.

❧ Help a child plant some seeds in a small container and place it in your kitchen window to sprout.

❧ Buy a meat thermometer. You'll use it often.

❧ Instead of buying regular applesauce, buy apples. A bowl of home-made applesauce with a sprinkle of cinnamon is a healthful, easy-to-make snack or dessert.

❧ Instead of putting the catsup bottle on the table, serve catsup in a little crock with a spoon. And don't forget to recycle the bottle.

❧ Just once during the summer, turn dinner into celebration time by serving sundaes or banana splits for your main meal. It's a lot less fattening than dinner *plus* banana splits, and one time won't ruin anyone's health.

❧ Take time today to smell the roses—and the soup!

Chapter 6

*In repentance and rest is your
salvation, in quietness and
trust is your strength.*

—Isaiah 30:15

The Secret of Stillness

*B*e still and know that I am God," the psalmist urges.
Easier said than done, right?

The complaint I hear from so many women these days is,
"I'm just dying for a little peace and quiet—a chance to relax
and to think and to pray. And somehow I just can't seem to
manage it."

"Stillness" is not a word that many of us even use any-
more, let alone experience. Yet women today, perhaps more
than at any other time in history, desperately need moments
of stillness. We are constantly on the move and stretched to
our maximum by all the hats we wear, all the balls we
juggle, and all the demands our lives bring. Part of enjoying
a beautiful home is seeking out opportunities to rest, plan,
regroup, and draw closer to God. And we do that when we
deliberately cultivate the beauty of stillness in our lives.

As I write these words, Bob and I are at a condo in the
California desert. It's July, and the temperature is 109
degrees. But the air is sparkling clear, and a breeze is ruffling
the palm tree fronds. As I gaze out over the rippling pool, a
deep sense of peace descends upon me.

We've just spent two days of rest, reading, and enjoying each other—letting our conversation roam to cover family, ministry, food, goals, God's love, his Word, and our writing. The conversation has quieted, and I can almost feel my bones relaxing as a sweet stillness steals over us.

Bob and I purposely set aside chunks of our yearly schedule just to be alone with each other and rethink our lives. We work hard all year, fulfilling many speaking engagements all over the country. Schedules, interviews, and travel keep us on the move. We have to make space for moments of stillness, or we would quickly lose track of each other...and grow out of touch with God.

> *Drop Thy still dews of quietness till all our strivings cease; take from our souls the strain and stress, and let our ordered lives confess the beauty of Thy peace.*
>
> —John Greenleaf Whittier

The door to stillness really is there waiting for any of us to open it and go through, but it won't open by itself. We have to choose to make being still a part of our lives.

I don't mean we need to be monks or hermits. The Scriptures tell us that if we are to live wisely, we must learn to balance the time we spend in quiet and calm with the time we spend in the fray of everyday existence. Ecclesiastes 3:1 says, "There is a time for everything." That includes a time and a place to cultivate a little stillness in the middle of your busy, productive life.

A Better Balance

I have not always appreciated the value of stillness the way I do now. In fact, I've always been the active, on-the-go type. But I'm 60-plus in years now, and a grandmother. Finally I am understanding the full importance of quiet times. And it's part of my privilege as a teacher of young women (see Titus 2:4) to share my growing appreciation of the value of stillness—to show how stillness can enrich our lives and replenish our spirits.

I've come to realize that all people need to get away from everything and everybody on a regular basis for thought, prayer, and rest. For me this includes both daily quiet times and more extended periods of relaxation and replenishment. And it includes both time spent with my husband and time spent with God. These times of stillness offer me the chance to look within and nurture the real me. They keep me from becoming frazzled and depleted by the world around me.

I would say the ideal balance between outward and inward pursuits should be about 50-50. By "outward" I mean working toward goals and deadlines, negotiating needs and privileges, coping with stress, taking care of daily chores, striving toward retirement—getting things done. "Inward" things include tuning in to my spiritual self, talking to God, exploring the sorrows, hopes, and dreams that make up the inner me, and just relaxing in God's eternal presence.

When I was younger, my life was tilted more outward and less inward. As I grow and mature (and perhaps reach another stage of my life), I find I'm leaning more toward the inward. I want my life to be geared more toward heaven. I want to lift my life, my hands, my head, and my body toward God, to spend more time alone with him—talking, listening, and just being. I want to experience the fragrance of his love and let that love permeate my life, to let the calmness of his spirit replenish the empty well of my heart, which becomes depleted in the busyness and rush of the everyday demands and pressures.

I want those things for you too. That's why I urge you: Do whatever is necessary to nurture quiet moments in your life. Don't let the enemy wear you so thin that you lose your balance and perspective. Regular time for stillness is as important and necessary as sleep, exercise, and nutritious food.

Making Time

But I know the objection that is already bubbling up in your mind: Who has time?

It's a common complaint—and a valid one.

It's true that the battle is on between Satan and the spirit of stillness. (The father of lies absolutely thrives on chaos and misery!) And it really isn't easy to eliminate all the distractions—the dust, the dirty clothes, the orders that need filling; timers buzzing, phones ringing, children needing us.

But here's what I've discovered: People who find time for stillness are people who have the energy and perspective to stay on top of their hectic "outer" lives.

And we're not alone as we struggle to find time for stillness. I truly believe that if we just recognize our daily need, God will open the doors to discovering ways to implement quiet times.

Anne Ortlund, whose books on the godly life have influenced a generation of Christian women, tells of a time when she had three children under three and not a spare moment in her day. Desperate for a time of quiet with the Lord, she tried desperate measures:

> Normally I sleep like a rock, but I said, "Lord, if you'll help me, I'll meet you from two to three A.M." I kept my tryst with him until the schedule lightened; I didn't die, and I'm not sorry I did it. Everybody has twenty-four hours. We can soak ourselves in prayer, in his Word, in himself, if we really want to.[1]

With God's help, we can do whatever we really want to do and make time for whatever we feel is a priority in our lives. What would do it in your life? Could you reduce TV time by 25 percent? Could you get up 15 minutes earlier or stay up half an hour later to take advantage of a quiet house? Could you trade off meal preparation in return for babysitting? With creativity and God's help, you can make space for stillness.

Perhaps the most important means of making time for stillness is the most obvious: Schedule it! Most of us have a tendency to schedule time for work, chores, errands, and family but leave our quiet time to happenstance. What happens? We manage to take care of work, chores, errands, and family, but somehow the quiet time falls by the wayside.

One friend of mine attended a one-day professional seminar at a cost of $250. I was eager to find out what was the one most important thing she had learned. She reported that this high-level course had taught her two important things: 1) Make a "to do" list, and 2) on that list, schedule quality time alone each day.

No one else can do it for you; *you* are the one who must make it and take it for yourself. Purposefully make yourself unavailable to the rest of the world each day and be available to God, yourself, and ultimately to others.

It doesn't have to be a large block of time. Fifteen minutes here and there can save you. Try getting up 15 minutes earlier so you can be utterly alone—or, if you're a night owl, stay up after everyone else is in bed. Ask a neighbor to watch the kids for just half an hour while you lock the bathroom door, sprinkle a few bath crystals in the tub, and enjoy a time of solitude and relaxation. Stake out a table in a quiet coffee shop in between carpool expeditions—or park your car under a quiet tree and enjoy a time of communion with God.

Whenever possible, try to schedule longer quiet times too. Author and speaker Florence Littauer travels all over the world, yet she will schedule an extra day here and there just to be alone. She orders room service and just enjoys her time reading, thinking, journaling...and just spending time with God. I've learned this from Florence and on occasion will do the same thing. I call it my "catch-up" day—time alone to journal, read magazines and newspaper articles, and do other things that refresh my mind and relieve tension. My favorite thing to do for myself is to listen to classical music or praise strings, put on a beauty mask, crawl up on our bed, and read *Today's Christian Woman* or *Shine* magazines.

If you have small children, such a "day off for stillness" may seem like an impossible dream. Even 15 minutes of solitude may seem out of reach. And I will admit that those years when little ones have first rights on your time can be a challenge. I know you can't schedule preschoolers, and help is often hard to find.

And yet...there really are ways to nurture the spirit of stillness even in the midst of the lovable chaos these tiny ones can put into your life.

I have to giggle every time I think of what my daughter Jenny used to do to give herself some quiet time. With three children aged two, four, and six, it was pretty difficult to find time for herself. So she put a beauty mask on her face and the faces of all three children. She used a green mud-type mask because the girls loved to have green faces with white eyes and rosy lips. Then all three children lay face-up on one bed. They knew their mask would crack if they talked or smiled or wiggled, so they lay very still. Jenny then got on the bed with a magazine and put on soft music, and they all relaxed. Often the children would go to sleep. I was amazed that it really worked.

Another day when the children were driving Jenny crazy about 4:30 in the afternoon (the disaster hour), Jenny stripped off their clothes and put all three in a bubble bath. Then she darkened the bathroom, lit a candle, sprayed some cologne, and sat down on the floor to read her Bible. I know it was God who calmed these cute monkeys down and gave Jenny a few moments of stillness. Now the children often ask mom for a bubble bath with candlelight.

After all, children benefit from stillness too. Small ones may seem to generate chaos, but immature nervous systems and bodies weary from the work of growing get the rest they need in an environment of order and peace. We do our children a favor when we teach them to find the spirit of stillness within themselves and make it a part of their lives.

This Time's for You

Does all of this sound like too much work? Does a quiet time sound like one more "should" in your life—something you ought to be doing but just can't manage? Or do you have a hard time justifying a time out for quiet when so many people depend on you, when so much needs to be done, when our whole culture glorifies action and busyness rather than quiet and contemplation?

If any of these arguments hold you back, keep reminding yourself that stillness is neither an impossible luxury nor an unreasonable demand—it's a necessity. You need times of quiet in order to have the inner resources to take care of the business of your life. Instead of a burden, let stillness be God's gift to you—the most lovely and healing "should" in your day.

If your rich uncle called and told you he was sending you a check for a thousand dollars but you had to go to the post office to pick it up, wouldn't you make the effort to get there? Your daily times of prayer and meditation and the more extended periods you set aside for the Lord really are worth the effort you put into making them happen. These intimate times with Jesus will plant seeds that grow and flower into the desires of your heart.

There are some things that can only be accomplished as we meet with the Lord in quiet. It is in communing with him that we get a handle on so many challenging parts of our lives—unpredictable emotions, worries and apprehensions, needs for approval and reassurance, fears and insecurities, hopes and dreams. It is during these special moments of our lives that we move toward getting things settled with God. Maybe that's why Paul advised the Thessalonians, "Make it your ambition to lead a quiet life...so that your daily life may win the respect of outsiders and so that you will not be dependent on anybody" (1 Thessalonians 4:11-12).

People who allow themselves time for stillness have made many exciting discoveries—about themselves, about God, and about the kind of life God has in mind. And these people seem to be calm and peaceful and generally have life in perspective. Their homes are often beautiful blends of activity and repose. And that's what I want for my life.

A Place for Stillness

Making space in your schedule for quiet meditation is absolutely vital to infusing your life with a little stillness, but serenity involves more than a chunk of your schedule. You can also nurture stillness by the way you relate to others and by the way you arrange your activities and environment.

Make a point of putting yourself in places that help you slow down, tune out the clamor, and listen to the quiet. Discover places that foster the stillness in your soul— garden, bathroom, chapel, library, cafe or coffeehouse, terrace, ocean, lake, mountain, or hammock—and go there regularly.

If you don't know about such a place, ask God to lead you to one. Remember, ours is the God who leads us beside still waters. If we ask, he will take us somewhere that restores our souls.

The outdoors, especially, can wonderfully nurture and quiet your soul. There's nothing like the sun and the breeze on your face or the sound of flowing water to calm your spirit and prepare you for stillness. And you don't have to sit for hours to enjoy the serenity of nature.

In fact, I find that physical exercise actually helps me achieve a quiet spirit. When I smell orange blossoms as I stride along, I invariably end up thinking and praying and praising. At the same time, something slows inside me. It's almost as if moving my feet helps bring the stillness to my soul.

Closer to home, you can nurture stillness in your home and garden. Soft fabrics and carpets reduce noise levels and thus foster serenity. Reducing clutter helps instill a sense of peace and order as well as reduce the urge to be "up and doing" all the time. Quiet corners and private crannies—a lawn chair out under the trees, a chair and a lamp in the corner behind a screen, even a beanbag chair in the basement—can serve as invitations to enjoy a moment of quiet.

Decorate your home with repose and serenity in mind. Soft colors—blues and greens especially—have been shown to have a calming effect on the spirit. Plants and vegetation add an air of peace. Soft, nonobtrusive music or one of those "nature" recordings of gentle rain or flowing streams can screen out more disturbing noises. A folding screen, a room divider, or a door that closes can foster the sense of getting away.

And, of course, cultivating a serene, godly spirit in yourself does a lot to create an atmosphere of stillness for your home. When you can, keep your voice low and gentle.

Respect the privacy and space of those who live with you and visit you. With a little care, the spirit of stillness can infuse your entire life and bless the lives of those whose lives touch yours.

The healing influence of stillness is more precious than ever today, when noise and clamor seem to close in on us from all sides. Most of us work, play, or go to school to a constant background of traffic and TV. We fight crowds at the mall, in restaurants, and on the highway; life seems more competitive and stressful than ever before. To people who are overstimulated and worn down by the constant barrage of modern living, seeking and finding stillness can be a literal lifesaver.

Your Private Haven

With all this in mind, it seems natural to look at the bedroom as the place in our homes where stillness can reign most beautifully. Most of us spend an average of ten hours a day in our bedrooms dressing, undressing, exercising, reading, reflecting, sewing, writing, puttering, talking on the telephone, watching television, playing with children, sleeping, eating, putting on makeup, and so on. At this rate we spend approximately half of our life in the bedroom. And we spend one-third of our lives actually in bed.

If at all possible, therefore, this room should be your most beautiful private sanctuary. It should be the first room you decorate, making it all you wish it to be. Your bedroom is your refuge, your trauma center, the scene of your most intimate moments, your most private retreat. It should be serene, with a quiet and gentle feeling—a place that invites you to stillness.

Don't neglect the room in your home where you express your love, your joys, your sorrows, and your times with Almighty God. This is not just a room where you go to sleep. It is a sanctuary where you escape and refill your spirit with God's Word and love.

In many homes I visit, I find that the bedroom is off-limits to guests. It has become the place to stockpile papers, sewing, business, ironing, typing—whatever is swept out of sight in cleaning the more public rooms. Dressers are piled high, the television is blaring, and toys clutter the floor. Sometimes there is a crib, a playpen, or a baby swing.

I know that not every woman has the luxury of enough room to house all the stuff she needs. Let me just urge you, if at all possible, to clean out your bedroom and turn it into a sanctuary of quiet and loveliness—a retreat where you can have peace to dream your dreams and nurture the benefits of stillness.

Developing the feel and atmosphere is so important. I believe it's totally worthwhile to put your energies into getting your bedroom to feel right. Your bedroom can be rich, whimsical, feminine, sentimental, luxurious, spiritual, and sensuous—a feeling that no one else can share but you and, if you are married, your mate.

I've worked hard to make Bob's and my bedroom a place of serenity, quiet, and peace for both of us. One of the first things we did was agree to remove the television set. I do not even need to tell you the disadvantages of this item in a bedroom. With it gone, we are now reading, listening to beautiful music, making love more often, praying, and enjoying times of beauty and joy.

But Bob and I have done more than remove the TV to make our bedroom a haven of stillness. Our bedroom was dark and sad when we first moved into our home. The dark paneled walls and dark hardwood floors gave off such a lonely feeling. So we painted the ceiling white, ripped out the small window, and put in ten feet of white-painted French doors. The frames of the other windows were painted white, and immediately the room was opened up to light and brightness. We added a light-patterned area rug and embellished our tall four-poster bed with a floral comforter that I rotate annually with an Amish quilt. One wall smiles with our family portraits, and a round table is covered with Battenberg lace and more family photos. The white Battenberg dust ruffle echoes the clean white feeling of the doors and windows. Over our bed are wall lamps to read by and a floral festoon of bright silk flowers with satin ribbons.

My nightstand is a small, old oak table with tall legs covered with a cross-stitched white cloth. It holds a Bible, fresh flowers, and an oil lamp. Bob's side has a stronger, more masculine look. On a small, desklike table rest a radio, his books, a green plant, and sometimes a pile of magazines and articles he's trying to plow through.

Bob and I have had many happy times in our room, and some difficult, heart-hurting times as well. But our memories always bring smiles of the beautiful times when we've shared the true spirit of stillness, the spirit of peace.

You don't have to be an interior designer, nor even hire one, to make your bedroom a welcoming, restful place. Just ask yourself what type of atmosphere you want to create. A garden of soft blues and greens? Bright colors that give you energy? Perhaps a warm collage of rusts, golds, and greens? Whatever the colors, make it the happiest room in your world.

Let your five senses lead you, and include whatever quiets and relaxes you. Consider the feel of the sheets— cool cotton or cozy flannel. Scent the air with potpourri or candles. A warm afghan or lap quilt tossed over the end of the bed or on a chair to pull over you while you nap will help you feel cozy. A good lamp by the bedside will invite you to read in bed. A radio or CD player near the bed will lift your spirits with beautiful music.

Think of your bedroom as a haven, a place to go for a quiet rest where you can kick off your shoes and shed the tight clothing and stress of the day. Think of it as a room where you'd like to retire or spend half your life relaxing. Once, during weeks of recovery after major surgery, I spent most of every day in our bedroom. I so looked forward to coming home from the hospital to crawl into our soft ruffled sheets. That's the spirit you want for your bedroom. Turn on soothing, spiritual music and enjoy your retreat, truly realizing the value of the time spent in soaking up a little stillness.

Simple Secrets

❧ Rearrange your bedroom furniture so that the first thing you see as you enter is the bed. Rejoice in the sense of welcome.

❧ A made-up bed is always more welcoming and relaxing than a tangle of sheets. Make a rule in your house that the last one out of the bed makes it up. If you rebel at wrestling with layers of sheets, blankets, and bedspreads, simplify matters with a comforter or a duvet.

❧ Clutter wearies the spirit and fights against serenity. At the very least, take 15 minutes to dejunk the room where you spend your quiet time.

❧ Shortly before your family comes home, take a minute to create a serene atmosphere. Clear the clutter in the living room or entry hall, light candles, put on soft music. And call a moratorium on problems and "discussions" for the next 30 minutes. If you live alone, give yourself half an hour of rest before tackling the evening chores.

❧ Keep a Bible, writing paper, and a pen on your bedside table for spiritual food during still moments. If you run a lot of errands, keep a Bible or an inspirational book in your car.

❧ When decorating for stillness, remember that it doesn't have to be done all at one time. It has taken us more than 36 years to be where we are now.

❧ Read Ecclesiastes 3—the whole chapter. List from that chapter what time in life it is for you now. What percentage of your life is available for inward pursuits?

❧ Make a list of sounds, smells, and places that tend to trigger a sense of stillness in you. Use that list as a guide in cultivating the spirit of stillness in your quiet time and in your home.

❧ If at all possible, consider a weekend retreat. Ask your minister or someone on your church staff about retreat centers available to you. A weekend in a beautiful setting with Bible, notebook, and helpful reading can yield huge benefits of stillness in your life.

❧ Try setting aside a "quiet corner" at home with books, comfortable cushions, and warm light. Make a family agreement to make stillness a priority for anyone in that place.

❧ Don't be afraid to take time out for quiet when things get too much. Unless your children are very small, set a timer for 15 minutes and disappear into bedroom or bathroom. Read your Bible or simply lie still and *be*.

❧ Children need stillness too. Try to make sure that every child in your home has a place where he or she can go to get away from the bustle and just be quiet. If your children share a room, try equipping the bottom of a closet with a beanbag chair and a large flashlight. If you have a large tree, a treehouse makes a wonderful place for thinking and dreaming.

❧ If you work outside the home, try setting aside your lunch hour as a time for stillness. Take a walk somewhere quiet and lovely. Drive to a park or find a quiet corner in a restaurant—or go home. Read, pray, and return to your job refreshed.

❧ Remember, the times when you feel you can't afford to slow down are the times you need moments of stillness most desperately. Let your impatience be a signal that it's time to get quiet.

❧ If you find it difficult to develop the habit of a quiet time, find a prayer partner with the same problem. Make a pact to hold each other accountable for six weeks of daily quiet time.

Chapter 7

God is so big He can cover the whole world with His love, and so small He can curl up inside your heart.

—June Masters Bacher

The Secret of Godliness

*B*onnie, the wife of the late composer and songwriter Johnny Green, tells of a time when she and her husband were living in London. They rented a beautiful, castle-like home so that he could enjoy privacy while writing the music for a new show—*Oliver.*

Bonnie, a new Christian, looked forward to spending this time with her Jewish husband while she grew in her faith. At four o'clock every afternoon, Bonnie would climb four flights of stairs with a tray of tea and crumpets to share with Johnny and his secretary.

But one day, as she approached the door that opened to the music room, she overheard words that struck daggers through her heart. Johnny and his secretary were professing their love to each other. Bonnie stood frozen on the landing as her dreams seemed to tumble down around her. "Oh, God!" she cried out in her heart, "What am I to do?"

In that instant she was aware of an answer: "Do nothing," the Lord told her in her heart. "Don't say a word; just continue to grow in me." And then, as strangled protests arose within her, she felt the gentle reassurance: "I will be with you."

The next two years put Bonnie through a crash course in godliness. Before long Johnny was spending four days a week with her and three days with the other woman. Bonnie said nothing. Instead, she found a Christian support group who prayed with her and loved her. At home, her bathroom became her prayer closet. Daily she prayed, cried, read her Bible, and leaned on God's strength. Again and again she claimed God's promise: "I will be with you." Sometimes she didn't think she could go on. But moment by moment she made the decision to keep on obeying.

In the 24 months that followed, the Lord gradually transformed Bonnie. But as the Greens' time in London drew to an end, she still didn't know where she stood in their marriage.

One day as Bonnie was packing for the long trip home, Johnny surprised her by asking, "Why do you think we should stay married?" At that point Bonnie poured out her heart to him. Today she is not really sure what she said. God's Spirit spoke through her, and for the next 15 minutes she shared her love with Johnny.

When she had finished, silence filled the room. Then Johnny said softly, wonderingly, "A man would have to be a fool to walk away from such a love as you have for me." In just a few minutes, two years of leaning on God bore fruit in the form of renewed love and devotion between the two of them.

But the best was yet to come! In 1977 Johnny personally met the Messiah and accepted him as Savior. And every day after that, in their beautiful Beverly Hills home, he and Bonnie had a Bible study together while he shaved in the bathroom. (Remember where Bonnie's prayer closet had been?) They prayed together and held many special spiritual conversations. By the time of his death, they were growing together daily in Christ.

A Transforming Spirit

No, I am not saying we will always get exactly what we want if we trust and obey God (although what he gives us may surpass anything we've ever dreamed of). I'm certainly not saying that every non-Christian or cheating husband will eventually come around if his wife prays (although I've seen such prayers bear wonderful fruit). But regardless of what happens in our lives, godliness can transform us into the lovely women God created us to be.

Think of it.

If your house is bursting at the seams with small children and chaos is nipping at your heels...a godly spirit can create a haven of order and calm.

If your nest is empty and your steps seem to echo in the silence...a godly spirit can fill that emptiness with relationship.

If your career or your relationships seem to be falling apart...a godly spirit can help your feet find the right path.

Or if you're just mired in the dailiness of living—another phone call to answer, another dish to wash, another weed to pull—seeking after godliness can help you focus on the eternal dimensions of what you're doing and gain a sense of doing these mundane tasks to the glory of God.

To me, a godly woman is one who possesses inner peace and tranquility; she doesn't have to prove herself to anyone. She is strong, and yet she doesn't use her strength to control or dominate people; neither does she depend on recognition from others. Hers is an inner contentment and satisfaction based not on accomplishments, position, or authority, but on a deep awareness of God's eternal and personal love for her.

That kind of inner peace, strength, confidence, and tranquility comes from depending on God, obeying him, drawing on his strength and wisdom, and learning to be like him. When this happens in our lives, we gradually grow free of anxious competitiveness and aggressiveness. We have no need to prove our worth and value because we *know* how much we are worth in God's sight. And then we are free to reach out in love to others.

I've seen that spirit at work in the lives of so many beautiful Christian women—women of all ages and every walk of life. I think of Lori, who was 25 when I first met her at the Edmonton airport in Alberta, Canada. In the two days we spent together then, I could see a godly spirit shining in the life this young lady. She had a vision for her family and the women of her church to become more Christ-centered, and that vision was contagious. We've been back several times to give our "More Hours in My Day" seminars, and each time Lori and her committee have beautifully organized exciting, creative times together.

I also think of the lovely 92-year-old woman who attended one of my seminars a few years back. This amazing lady sat through all four sessions, scribbling notes the entire time. I remember thinking, "At 92, who even cares?" But this new friend told me she wanted to learn everything she could in life so she could pass on her learning to younger women. Her teachable spirit humbled and blessed me. I only hope that when I am 92 I will be as eager to learn and to grow in God's grace.

Godly values—spiritual awareness, obedience, trust, self-giving love—are so different from the values that seem to run this worldly age. And yet God's strategy for growth and happiness has been around for almost 2000 years. Countless generations of women who have taken his plan seriously have found that it works. I pray that we might take it seriously as well, growing daily in godliness and allowing godliness to beautify our homes and lives.

Growing in Godliness

Becoming a woman of God begins with making a personal commitment to Jesus Christ. Only he can give us the strength to change. Only he can give us the fresh start that allows godliness to grow strong in us.

Second Corinthians 5:17 reminds us, "If anyone is in Christ, he is a new creation; the old has gone, the new has come!" That's what I discovered many years ago when I, a 16-year-old Jewish girl, received Christ into my heart. My life began to change from that moment on, and the years since then have been an exciting adventure.

It hasn't always been easy. I've had to give up much bitterness, anger, fear, hatred, and resentment. Many times I've had to back up and start over, asking God to take control of my life and show me his way to live. But as I learned to follow him, God has guided me through times of pain and joy, struggle and growth. And how rewarding it has been to see the spirit of godliness take root and grow in my life! I give thanks and praise for all his goodness to me over the years.

I'm not finished yet—far from it. Growing in godliness is a lifelong process. And although God is the one who makes it possible, he requires my cooperation. If I want his godliness to shine in my life and beautify my home, I must be willing to change what God wants me to change and learn

> *If each moment is sacred—a time and place where we encounter God—life itself is sacred.*
>
> —Jean M. Blomquist

what he wants to teach me. How? Here are some of the ways I've learned to keep myself open to the spirit of godliness.

Stay in Tune with God

God's Word is the foundation of my security and strength. Only through daily immersion in Scripture and through daily prayer and meditation can I tap in to God's strength and love and get a handle on what he wants for my life.

Because I sometimes need a nudge to keep these disciplines regular and meaningful, I have a habit of keeping a prayer basket close at hand. This pretty little carryall (I like to use a soft, heart-shaped basket in pastel colors) gathers together in one place the tools I need to keep in regular touch with God. My prayer basket contains:

1. *A Bible* to prepare my mind and heart to communicate with God.

2. *A daily devotional* or other inspirational reading.

3. *My prayer planner* (more on this later).

4. *A bunch of silk flowers* to remind me of the beauty and fragrance of the Lord Jesus himself.

5. *A small box of tissues* for the days I cry in joy or pain.

6. *A pen* for journaling my prayers and writing notes.

7. *A few pretty postcards or notecards* for when I feel moved to communicate God's love to someone I'm praying for.

Seeing my basket waiting for me is a wonderful invitation to times of prayer and a reminder when I haven't taken the time to pray. And it is so convenient to pick up and take to my prayer closet for a quiet time of communion with my heavenly Father.

Where is my closet? It may be a different place every day. (That's the beauty of the portable prayer basket.) Sometimes I settle down at my desk for a quiet time with God. Other times I use the bed, the breakfast room table, the bathtub, a chair by the fireplace, the front yard by the pond, or a shady spot under a tree—anywhere where I can enjoy privacy.

The actual content of my devotional times varies according to how much time I have available. But generally I start by reading a brief inspirational message or prayer. Then I open my Bible and read a chapter or more. (If time is really short, it may be only a verse.)

Next, I turn to my prayer planner. This is a tool I developed many years ago to help me remember prayer requests and pray more effectively for others. My prayer planner is a simple loose-leaf notebook divided into seven sections—one for each day of the week. I've divided all the people and projects I want to pray for—family, friends, church, finances, and so on—into the various sections. For instance, I reserve Mondays to pray for my family, Tuesdays for my church and its servants and activities, Wednesdays for my personal concerns, and so on. (I reserve Sunday for sermon notes and outlines.) Organizing my prayer times in this way helps keep me from being overwhelmed while helping me remember to be faithful in my prayer life.

I have filled my prayer planner with photos of people I'm praying for, information about their interests and needs, and special things to remember about them. When I receive prayer requests, I assign them a place in my prayer planner. I also go through my planner from time to time and weed out old requests so I don't become overwhelmed. This little book has become a creative, colorful companion that is so close to my heart.

In the back of my prayer planner, I keep a supply of blank paper for journaling my prayers. This has not been an easy habit for me to develop. I do so much writing for magazine articles, books, and letters that more writing feels a little like work. But for the past few years I have made the effort to write down my praise, my confession, my thanks, and my requests. I give the Lord my hurts, my pain from the past, my disappointments, and all the questions my mind can think of—in writing. I also write down the convictions of what I hear God saying to me. I'm learning firsthand the benefits of putting my conversations with God in written form:

1. *I am able to verbalize things I've held in my heart but never spoken about.* The act of writing somehow seems to bring up my thoughts, feelings, and desires and expose them to the light of God's love.

2. *Writing out my confessions helps me get honest with the Lord.* Somehow a confession feels more real when it's down there in black and white. But this means that God's forgiveness feels more real too.

3. *I can see concrete evidence of my spiritual life*—and my spiritual growth—when I read back over past prayers.

4. *My faith grows as I see God's answers more clearly*— God's "yes," "no," and "wait." Writing down the answers I think I hear helps me discern which ones really are of God.

5. *My obedience is strengthened.* Once again, written promises are harder to ignore than mental ones. Once I have written down my sense of what God wants me to do, I am more likely to follow through.

There is another kind of writing that I often do during my prayer times. Often while I am praying, God will bring to mind someone who needs my love or care. That's what the notecards are for. When God brings someone to mind, I try to stop right there and drop that person a line, assuring him or her of God's love and my prayers. Having the materials right there at hand makes this encouraging habit easy to maintain.

Stick Close to God's People

My one-on-one times with God are essential to my growth in godliness, but they alone are not enough. I'm convinced that we were never meant to live a godly life in a vacuum. To grow in godliness, we need to share love and support and prayers with our sisters and brothers in Christ.

The New Testament makes it clear that Christ's people are meant to function as a body—praying together, enjoying one another, working together to do Christ's business in the world. This means that unless we are plugged into a fellowship of fellow believers we are incomplete—just as lifeless and as useless as a severed hand or foot.

Our earliest record of the way God's people went about their lives gives a picture of Christians growing in godliness with other Christians: "They devoted themselves to the apostles' teaching and to the fellowship, to the breaking of bread and to prayer....Every day they continued to meet together in the temple courts. They broke bread in their homes and ate together with glad and sincere hearts, praising God and enjoying the favor of all the people" (Acts 2:42, 46-47).

What an exciting picture of the kind of atmosphere that fosters godliness. To me, it's a picture of the kind of involvement I need with other Christians if I want godliness to permeate my life and beautify my home.

Being involved in a vital, Bible-centered church is one way I try to stay close to the body. Meeting for public worship, supporting missions and others' projects of love, gathering for times of learning and fellowship—all of these activities help reinforce godliness in our lives. But "body life" happens in smaller groups, too—"wherever two or three are gathered" (Matthew 18:20). In fact, some of our most important growing happens when small groups gather in the name of Christ to pray, study, and have fellowship together.

Some of my most precious moments of Christian fellowship have happened within my own family—times of sharing with Bob over breakfast, sweet times of prayer as I tucked a child into bed, unexpected conversations as we worked together in the kitchen or the garden.

And what blessings have come when five or six of us have gathered for a home Bible study or a time of prayer! It is during those intimate gatherings that we really "got down to business" in our lives——loving and encouraging one another and holding one another to accountability for growth in Christ. I have prayed and wept and laughed and hugged over many a cup of afternoon tea while the spirit of godliness filled the very air.

What a privilege to worship together, pray together, work together, and grow together with our fellow Christians! What a joy to support one another in times of crisis and need. Such amazing things happen when we choose to reach out to one another, sustaining one another in love.

When our daughter's close friend, Lynn, began her battle with cancer, I decided to have a small luncheon for her before she entered the City of Hope hospital for her bone-marrow transplant, which would end in 40 days of isolation. Five of us sat around our breakfast room table eating delicious Cobb salads and warmed croissants, and then we topped off the meal with yogurt-and-fresh-fruit parfaits.

But we weren't finished yet. The dishes were cleared and replaced by a scattering of colored marking pens and five sheets of paper. At my direction, Lynn traced her hand onto the paper. (No one yet knew what this was all about.) Step two was to give each guest a paper with

Lynn's "handprint" on it. Lynn kept one, which would ultimately be given to her husband, Walt. We each drew a small heart in the hand outlined on our paper. Then our creative hands colored the handprinted paper any way we wanted.

And here's the exciting part. Now each of us placed one hand on Lynn's hand and one hand on our paper hand as we prayed for Lynn's healing and her future. We took these handprints home and placed them on the refrigerator door. Every time we passed or opened that door, we would place our hand over Lynn's, and our hearts would beat together as we prayed for her.

That was many years ago at this writing, and Lynn is now living a healthy and normal life. She tells us that our support and prayers made all the difference during her surgery and recovery. But she was not the only one to benefit! Each one of us experienced God's loving hands and arms around us as we helped support our friend through a time of crisis. We are now a part of the blessings too.

Godliness, in other words, is contagious! Its source is God, but we also catch it from one another as we intimately share our lives. And one of the most important ways we can share is to pass on what we have learned about living in Christ to those who are newer to the adventure than we are. Titus 2:3-5 advises older women to teach the younger women in love, self-control, purity, industriousness, kindness, and true loveliness. To me, this means putting myself in situations where the contagious spirit of godliness is most likely to be spread to those younger than I am.

When our children were growing up, I wanted them to see me on my knees in prayer. I wanted them to be around as I gave to and received from other women scriptural counsel and prayer support. I wanted them to see the notes of encouragement I wrote and sent to those who were hurting. Sure, I talked about God. Bob and I made sure our children were educated in Scripture. We made prayer and church attendance part of the regular routine that we required of our children. And yet these were not the ways that a godly spirit moved from one generation to another in our family. The most important lessons in godliness we gave our children were transmitted as we grew in godliness ourselves.

Of course, that's how we caught the spirit in the first place. When I was about 26 years old, our little family moved to Newport Beach, California. Newport Beach is a lovely and affluent town—full of sailboats, yachts, and beautiful people. But to me the most beautiful people of all were four older women who took me under their wing and drew me into their Tuesday morning prayer group. For four years I sat with those women as they took God's Word and implemented it in their lives. I remember thinking, "That's the kind of woman I want to be," and in the years that followed I have tried to draw from their example.

Now, many years later, my four friends in Newport are still doing what they were doing during the years that they taught me—still drawing younger women into their midst, teaching and loving them and modeling what being a godly woman is all about. Theirs is a wonderful heritage of godliness that they are passing along to yet another generation. I only hope I am doing the same.

Remember Who's in Charge

We humans are made in such a way that we learn best by doing. That's true in so many areas of our life, and it's especially true when it comes to being God's people. We grow in godliness as we hear God's word to us through Scripture and prayer and our fellow Christians—and then act in obedience to that word.

This means that when I hear that little inner voice tell me I've been neglecting my prayer times, I don't rationalize and make excuses. I grab my prayer basket and find a quiet corner.

It means that when someone's name keeps coming to mind during my prayer times, I don't just dismiss the experience. I call that person just as soon as I say "amen."

It also means that when I pick up my Bible and read "love your enemies" or "give to the needy" or "do not steal," I take those commandments seriously, and I pay heed to the spirit of those words, not just the letter of the law. To be more specific, I make our tithe a priority item in our budget. If Bob and I quarrel, I do what is necessary to straighten things out before bedtime. When a friend or a relative slights me, I love that person anyway.

But how difficult obedience can be when my heart is wrenched with pain and anger...or when I just can't see the light at the end of the tunnel. The normal human response is to fight back against all the wrongs and "not fairs" or just to give up in weariness. Sometimes it takes a monumental effort of the will just to hang on in trust and obedience.

That is why we need to stay plugged in to God through prayer and Scripture study. That's why we need the embracing love of our brothers and sisters in Christ. And that's why, most of all, we need to remember that we are never meant to obey in our own strength.

After all, obedience is only obedience when someone else is in charge. God knows all about our pain, our failures, our frustrations. He knows about the relative who blames me for the family's problems, about the church group who stiffed me on my speaking fee, about the grocery store clerk who treated me rudely. He knows about my secret passion for chocolate, my judgmental attitude toward my neighbor, my repeated failures at keeping a quiet time with him. And he has promised to take care of me if I give all these circumstances of my life over to him.

Of course, that's the hardest step of all. Giving up control of my life is scary and painful, even when I'm perfectly aware that I'm not doing such a great job of running the show. Sometimes I may have to repeat that act of surrender several times a day. Sometimes I just have to tell him that I'm *willing* to surrender, but he will have to help me do it.

But what a wonderful discovery as I continue on that path of obedience, trusting in God and giving my life to him. That's when I learn what it means to allow godliness to grow in me and to allow its lovely fragrance to penetrate and transform every corner of my life, making me truly blessed.

Like Crystal in the Sun

The famous thirty-first chapter of Proverbs is a portrait of the kind of godly woman I want to be. She is hardworking, nurturing, creative. She has a good business sense as well as a finely tuned sense of balance and delight in her role as wife and mother. Most important, she is a "woman who fears the LORD" (Proverbs 31:30). And what is her reward for all her efforts? "Her children arise and call her blessed; her husband also, and he praises her" (verse 28).

Such a reward would warm any woman's heart. I know I love it whenever Bob and the children praise me and call me blessed. But I am also aware that many of you are godly women who pattern your life after biblical principles but do not receive praise from anyone. Many times you may feel or say, "What's the use? No one appreciates me."

Oh, there have been times in my life when I haven't felt appreciated, but God has taught me through these void periods of my life. I began to realize that God was dealing with me on the level of my motivations and my expectations. He wanted me to do whatever I did to please him, not my husband or my children or anyone else.

When I began to stop expecting people to react in a certain way, I began to act out of proper motivation. I was aiming to please God, not expecting certain behavior from family and friends.

Do you know what began to happen? When I stopped expecting praise from my family, I started getting it! My praise came about when my family was free to be themselves. However, I'm not nearly as hungry for compliments as I once was. I find I am satisfied because I am becoming more used to responding in a godly way to life and its many situations. I have become more aware of who I really am, God's child, and why I am here: to grow closer to him and learn his way of doing things. In the process, I have become far less dependent on other people to feel worthwhile.

In talking to hundreds of women each year, I have noticed that some of them are vainly trying to find the answer to those same two questions: "Who am I?" and "Why am I here?" If God's answer to these two basic questions of life is not yet engraved on your heart, I pray that you will set out on a journey to be satisfied with your answers. Go to God's Word, talk to a godly friend, attend a Bible-teaching church, and set aside a part of each day to talk to God in prayer. If you seek him sincerely, God will show you the traits of the godly woman he created you to be. Then step out in obedience, depending on Jesus. As you do, the beauty of godliness will begin to shine in your life.

I love what Bonnie Green says on her testimony tape:

> It is the glow within that creates beauty. People are like stained-glass windows. They sparkle like crystal in the sun. At night they continue to sparkle only if there is light from within.[1]

As women of godliness, we have the wonderful opportunity to let our lives sparkle with God's love. Almighty God is our guide and shepherd and will give us godliness that will permeate our lives and make our homes beautiful.

Simple Secrets

❧ Frame a card with your favorite Scripture verse and hang it next to your desk or sink. When you need a break, ponder it.

❧ If you like background music in the car, during exercise, or just around the house, tune in to a Christian station. I have found that music helps words of Christian comfort and encouragement get a toehold in my heart.

❧ Explore one of the classic books that have lifted the faith of so many Christians over the years. Oswald Chambers' *My Utmost for His Highest,* Hannah Whitehall Smith's *The Christian's Secret of a Happy Life,* or any of C.S. Lewis' books are wonderful places to start.

❧ Invest in more than one Scripture translation. Seeing various versions will help you get a clearer picture of the Bible's message to you.

❧ Volunteer your home for a Bible study or a small-group meeting. Thank God for the privilege of hosting an opportunity for two or three—or more—to gather in his name.

❧ Frame a family photo and put it in the bathroom. Pray each morning for your family as you brush your teeth, apply your makeup, or style your hair.

❧ Make sure your little ones have access to a good children's Bible and some wonderful, imaginative, Christ-centered books for kids. Read them aloud during your time together and talk about what they mean.

❧ Ask an acquaintance at church to be your prayer partner for a set period of time. Meet or call each other once a day to share concerns and pray together. Or exercise body and spirit and pray together as you take a walk.

❧ Be on the lookout for ways to obey God by serving others. This could mean something as simple as helping in the church nursery or as complex as volunteering to organize an emergency food pantry at your church. Listen for the Spirit's leading and then step out in obedience.

❧ If you are not in the habit of journaling your prayers, try doing it for an experimental period. Buy a lovely blank book or set aside a section of your notebook and commit to praying on paper for a period of six weeks. Once that time is up, you may not want to stop.

❧ As an alternative to writing your prayers, try drawing them or even singing them. Let the Spirit guide you in expressing yourself to God in the ways he has gifted you.

❧ Look for ways to turn your everyday activities into occasions for prayer and thanksgiving. As you scrub toilets or hose down the front stairs, ask God to use those mundane tasks to his glory. When you sit down to return a raft of phone calls, pray briefly for each person and ask God to bless his or her life through you. As you jog or ride your exercise bike, thank God for the gift of your body and the wonderful way you are made, no matter what your particular shape happens to be.

Chapter 8

There are few hours in life more agreeable than the hour dedicated to the ceremony known as afternoon tea.

—HENRY JAMES

The Secret of Hospitality

The "parlor" was tiny, just an extra room behind the store. But the tablecloth was spotless, the candles were glowing, the flowers were bright, the tea was fragrant. Most of all, the smile was genuine and welcoming whenever my mother invited people to "come on back for a cup of tea."

How often I heard her say those words when I was growing up. And how little I realized the mark they would make on me.

Those were hard years after my father died, when Mama and I shared three rooms behind her little dress shop. Mama waited on the customers, did alterations, and worked on the books until late at night. I kept house—planning and shopping for meals, cooking, cleaning, doing laundry—while going to school and learning the dress business as well.

Sometimes I felt like Cinderella—work, work, work. And the little girl in me longed for a Prince Charming to carry me away to his castle. There I would preside over a grand and immaculate household, waited on hand and foot by attentive servants. I would wear gorgeous dresses and entertain kings and queens who marveled at my beauty and my wisdom as they lavished me with gifts.

But in the meantime, of course, I had work to do. And although I didn't know it, I was already receiving a gift more precious than any dream castle could be. For unlike Cinderella, I lived with a loving mother who understood the true meaning of sharing and of joy—a mother who brightened people's lives with her gift of hospitality.

Our customers quickly learned that Mama offered a sympathetic ear as well as elegant clothes and impeccable service. Often they ended up sharing their hurts and problems with her. And then, inevitably, would come the invitation: "Let me make you a cup of tea." She would usher our guests back to our main room, which served as a living room by day and a bedroom by night. Quickly a fresh cloth was slipped on the table, a candle lit, fresh flowers set out if possible, and the teapot heated. If we had them, she would pull out cookies or a loaf of banana bread. There was never anything fancy, but the gift of her caring warmed many a heart on a cold night.

And Mama didn't limit her hospitality to just our guests. On rainy days I often came home from school to a hot baked potato, fresh from the oven. Even with her heavy workload, Mama would take the time to make this little Cinderella feel like a queen.

My mother's willingness to open her life to others—to share her home, her food, and her love—was truly a royal gift. She passed it along to me, and I have the privilege of passing it on to others. What a joy to be part of the warmth and beauty of hospitality!

Entertaining Angels

Hospitality is so much more than entertaining—so much more than menus and decorating and putting on a show. To me, it means organizing my life in such a way that there's always room for one more, always an extra place at the table or an extra pillow and blanket, always a welcome for those who need a listening ear. It means setting aside time for planned fellowship and setting aside lesser priorities for impromptu gatherings.

Sometimes we may feel that this "open model" of hospitality is not easy to follow. But it's not really optional for us who call ourselves Christians; the Bible tells us specifically to "cheerfully share your home with those who need a meal or a place to stay for the night" (1 Peter 4:9 TLB). And besides, the benefits of such a spirit of hospitality will sometimes circle around and touch us from behind when we least expect it.

During the early years of our marriage, when Bob was teaching fifth grade, we found built-in opportunities for hospitality in his students. Those ten-year-olds loved Mr. Barnes, and they were forever showing up to "help" us at home. I never knew when I would have extra hands for the dusting or an audience for my cooking. And when Bob went out to work in the yard, he nearly always had a troop of boys along. They would ride their bikes over to help or just to hang around—anything just to be near him.

One young boy named Jimmy seemed especially attached to Bob. He was always dropping by, so one evening we invited him for dinner. He stayed and stayed, obviously reluctant to leave. But eventually he did go home, and in time he passed on to the sixth grade and out of our lives.

Years passed. Then one day in 1990, Bob received a surprise phone call. "Little Jimmy"—now 45 years old—had been talking with some old friends at his high-school reunion. "Whatever happened to Mr. Barnes, our fifth-grade teacher?" they had wondered, and Jimmy had decided to find out.

It took many phone calls, including a couple to the Department of Motor Vehicles, but Jimmy finally found us—just 20 miles away! We chatted over the phone, and we found to our delight that he was pastoring a growing church in a neighboring community. His adorable wife, the mother of his four boys, invited us to dinner to reunite her husband with his favorite teacher. The gift of hospitality we had extended 35 years before was returning full circle to us.

But there was more. That evening, over dinner, we learned more about Jimmy's story. He had grown up in a troubled, alcoholic home. In those days when he was our constant visitor, he used to wish Bob could be his dad. In fact, on the night he came for dinner, he had pretended we were his family and that he lived with us. Even after our lives grew apart, the memory of our hospitality had stayed with him through many difficult drug and alcohol years. Gradually God had touched his heart, drawn him into the family of God, and prepared him for ministry.

> *Share your life, and find the finest joy man can know. Do not be stingy with your heart. Get out of yourself into the lives of others, and new life will flow into you—share and share alike.*
>
> —Joseph Fort Newton

That evening, as we left this wonderful, grown-up man of God, little Jimmy told his favorite teacher with tears in his eyes, "You were the only real dad I ever had, and I thank you."

That night Bob and I learned anew the wisdom of Hebrews 13:2: "Do not forget to entertain strangers, for by so doing some people have entertained angels without knowing it."

That, of course, is one of the great "side effects" of hospitality. When God's children are in need, we can be the ones to help them out—and the results of our caring can be beyond measure. We never know at the time whether we are God's instrument for changing a life. We may find out only years later, as we found out with little Jimmy. Or we may never know—in this lifetime. But we can know, when we "practice hospitality" (Romans 12:13), that we are living our lives the way God means for us to live—in openness, sharing, and love.

Nothing Fancy

Hospitality comes in many shapes, sizes, and colors. It's fun to be creative and flexible. Of course, not everyone feels comfortable with having guests. But if this discomfort is due at least in part to a lack of modeling and practice, it can be remedied. I guarantee you, the more you practice the spirit of hospitality, the easier it becomes.

And you really don't need elaborate preparations to share hospitality. The spirit of hospitality can thrive in the simplest of settings as long as we keep tuned in to its real purposes.

Bob and I received a dramatic reminder of that reality the year we moved into our barn. We were eager to share our new home with others, so we decided to have a Christmas open house for 50 friends. Being an organized person, I jumped the gun a bit and sent out invitations in October for our December date. But as the time for our open house drew near, we found ourselves far from ready. Our fall had been packed with holiday seminar bookings. We were exhausted. The house had yet to be decorated, and I hadn't even begun putting together the elaborate menu I had planned.

Decorating for Christmas is usually a fun time for us. We do it the weekend after Thanksgiving so we can enjoy the season as long as possible. But by December 7 that year, less than a week before the party, we found ourselves stressed and anxious, and not a decoration was up. At ten o'clock that evening, as we sat by the fire, I suggested to Bob that we pull out our boxes with the garlands and at least begin decorating the mantel—the beautiful, strong beam that stretched almost all the way across our "great room." To humor me, Bob got down the boxes, and we set about hanging the garlands.

Sitting on top of our mantel was a large, very heavy, hand-carved wooden goose. That evening, as the excitement of getting ready for Christmas began to lift my spirits, I began to talk to the goose. "What shall we do with you? Perhaps a big plaid bow around your neck—or maybe a wreath with twinkle lights would be fun…"

At that point the goose jumped off the mantel, breaking his neck and my right foot. That night ended with a trip to the emergency room.

The next day, with a glue gun and a bow, we managed to repair our goose and get him back on the mantel. But I was hobbling around in a cast, in a lot of pain, and worrying because we still had the house to decorate and a lavish buffet meal to prepare for our guests, who were due to arrive in a few days.

I was about to fall apart with anxiety when Bob beautifully suggested that we scratch the lavish buffet, reduce the event to casual, and serve my famous ten-bean soup, tossed green salad, and crusty French bread. "Great idea!" I exclaimed, and immediately relaxed enough to carry through with the decorating and the menu.

And what a wonderful evening it was for us and our guests! The Christmas table looked beautiful with its red plaid taffeta tablecloth, sparkling oil lamps, pine branches, shiny red and green apples, and opalescent sprinkles of "snow." Our tree sparkled with white twinkle lights, taffeta plaid bows, and the ornaments we've amassed over the years of our marriage. Green garlands bright with more twinkle lights and bows draped the room. Our white soup tureens steamed with the ten-bean soup. The green salad was fragrant with my father's famous olive oil dressing and cheery with red cherry tomatoes and freshly grated Parmesan cheese.

As our guests arrived, the aroma of cinnamon tea warmed the room—and our hearts. And do you know what? Not a single guest seemed worried that the lavish buffet had not materialized. Instead they raved, "What a great idea to serve soup! And it's delicious. Can we get the recipe?"

Little did they know that Bob and I had already bagged some beans and attached the recipe for each guest to take home with them. Our guests were delighted as we handed them their bags of beans, gave them a hug, and sent them off with a gift to share with their own families.

Hospitality, you see, can thrive in the humblest circumstances. It's a matter of opening our lives to others...giving them the best we have to offer, but never allowing elaborate preparations to substitute for true warmth and genuine care.

A Spontaneous Welcome

Sometimes it really is fun to throw an "event"—complete with written invitations, elaborate decorations, and lavish foods. And even a very formal dinner can be gracious and fulfilling—deeply satisfying and filled with a spirit of welcome. Your meticulous planning and loving preparation, your most beautiful tablecloths and place settings and centerpieces, all can be wonderful ways to tell your guests that you care enough to plan for their visit.

And yet we rob ourselves of joy when we limit our hospitality to what can be arranged in advance. We so enrich our lives when we get in the habit of spur-of-the-moment hospitality.

Does that idea strike terror in your heart? Do you envision your "angels" arriving to a messy house and an empty refrigerator? Then you're beginning to realize one of the secrets of hospitality: It can be spontaneous only when you've taken the time to prepare for it! It's wise to be ready and plan ahead for those who may show up at your door or you may decide to invite at the last minute.

That's one reason I organize my life to keep on top of the housework, making sure the house is more or less picked up and reasonably presentable. (The other reason is that I want to make my house a pleasant place for Bob and me to live in.)

That's one reason I keep silk and fresh flowers on hand and a supply of candles in the freezer. (In the freezer because candles stored that way don't drip or sputter. I always have them on hand because candles add a warm, welcoming glow, and candlelight is kind in hiding dusty baseboards or any other less-than-perfect household state.)

And that's also a reason I make a habit of cooking ahead. I try to have backups in my freezer or cupboard for those spontaneous invites. A jar of spaghetti sauce (homemade or not), a tamale pie casserole, frozen piecrust, powdered lemonade, olives, nuts, marinated artichokes, a jar of cookies—and I'm always ready for a quick tea party or dinner with old friends or unannounced "angels."

Robert Louis Stevenson said, "A friend is a present you give yourself." I have found that planning for spontaneous hospitality is one of the most important ways of giving that gift. Friendships are cultivated through spending time together. So we purposely plan to make that happen, whether the actual event is planned or not.

Room for Hospitality

We have always considered overnight guests a joy and an honor, especially since our children began leaving home and we've had space for a guest room. It's so much fun to give our guests the royal treatment in our princess room.

When our daughter, Jenny, was a little girl, she loved for me to read or tell her the story of "The Princess and the Pea." You remember, it's about the beautiful princess who was so sensitive that a single pea placed under 12 mattresses kept her awake at night. I think Jenny even tried this on her own bed. Because she loved this story so much, we started to call her our "princess," and her bedroom became the Princess Room.

After Jenny left for college and then married, we began using her room as our guest room. And people would always smile and get a little excited when we would exclaim, "You get to sleep in the Princess Room."

When we moved into our current home, our extra bedroom naturally became a Princess Room as well. And what fun we had decorating it for our overnight guests. Our current Princess Room has its own bath with Laura Ashley wallpaper and two rollout windows that let in a cool breeze. The bed, an old oak double, is topped with an Amish quilt in shades of pink, peach, and green and a pile of puffy white pillows. (I usually have a doll or a couple of teddy bears playing around the pillows.) A freshly starched lace cloth on the bedside table sets off an oil lamp and family photos, and built-in shelves hold books for guests from two to twenty. An old iron lamp with a frosted glass shade lights the way to reading in bed.

Best of all is a window seat with a Laura Ashley striped cushion to coordinate with the wallpaper. More pillows make the seat cozy and invite guests to relax and enjoy the view of trees and pond. The hardwood floor is softened with an Oriental area rug that echoes many of the colors in the room.

We hope we have created a comfortable, warm, and loving experience for our guests who sleep in the Princess Room. But—and this is very important—you don't have to have a special room in order to make your overnight guests feel special. I have stayed in many homes as I travel the country, and I can testify that little touches of caring and welcome can make even the most humble quarters inviting and hospitable.

After all, the key to successful hospitality is being sensitive to the needs of your guests. Even if your guest room is a pulled-out sofa bed or an air mattress on the floor, you can provide the little extras that say "I care." An extra mattress pad or "egg crate" cushion to make the bed more comfortable, a little basket of travel-sized soaps, shampoos, and lotions in the bathroom, a bowl of fruit, a clock radio tuned to a great local station, a stack of magazines or information on local attractions—any of these things can help your guests feel at home. And of course, a fragrant cup of coffee or steaming mug of cocoa on a tray in the morning makes anyone feel special—a wonderful affirmation of the joy of sharing your lives and making your home beautiful through hospitality.

Not Just for "Company"

The goal of hospitality is to make guests feel special and loved. But why should that effort be reserved only for "company"? I really believe true hospitality should be an everyday attitude in our homes—a commitment to sharing our lives with each other as well as our guests.

After all, what are we saying to our families, the most precious people in our lives, if we break out the candles and the flowers and the china only for special guests and serve the people we love on TV trays and paper plates?

A few summers ago while on vacation, my Bob injured his knee playing tennis. Several days after arriving home, Bob's knee pain became so bad that he actually decided to stay in bed for the morning. It was, at last, an opportunity for me to share hospitality and prepare breakfast in bed for my husband—something I often do for overnight guests.

I set out the tray with fresh hot coffee in a pretty china cup and saucer, steaming bran muffins, fruit and coconut, almond granola, fresh-squeezed orange juice from our own trees, a vase of freshly picked flowers, and a candle. The tray looked beautiful as I carried it into the bedroom, although I didn't know how Bob would respond to such a feminine-looking setup.

But as I puffed up the pillows and placed the tray on his lap, Bob's eyes spoke volumes to me. "How beautiful!" he exclaimed. "And just for me." For weeks after that I heard Bob tell family and friends about his breakfast in bed with flowers and candlelight.

I realized it was the first time in more than 35 years I had ever awakened my Bob, whom I love so deeply, with a beautiful breakfast tray. Since that occasion I've decided to do it more often, with or without sore knees.

I urge you to share the gift of hospitality with someone in your own family. I did, and I'm still hearing about it.

If you live alone, take the time to share a little hospitality with yourself. Resist the temptation to graze out of the refrigerator, fork up a microwave dinner from its cardboard container, or skip meals altogether. At least some of the time, take the trouble to prepare a meal, set a place at the table, and sit down in thanksgiving. (Better yet, put together a meal and invite a lonely neighbor over!) When you treat yourself like an honored guest, you will find yourself much better nourished in body and spirit—and encouraged to reach out to others as well.

A Heritage of Hospitality

Because I first caught the spirit of hospitality from my mother, I am acutely aware of how important it is to pass on this sharing attitude. I'm finding a lot of joy in teaching hospitality—not only in the seminars I hold, but to our granddaughter, Christine (our "princess in training"). Each year since she has been three years old, on her July 9 birthday we plan a tea party. This event has become a tradition we both anticipate eagerly—almost more than her birthday party.

The year Christine turned nine, she decided to invite her friend Leah to an "overnighter" at PaPa and Grammie's house. (The tea party would be the next day.) The girls were excited as their moms dropped them off at our house. They brought their favorite dolls, too, as special tea party guests. As soon as things were settled, we organized and talked about what was to happen. We sat at the breakfast bar off our kitchen, and I had the girls make a list of the coming events.

The girls decided to bake cookies for the party the night before so they would have more time the day of the party to prepare and enjoy the occasion. As soon as our plans were mapped out, we started in on the cookies.

Christine and I have been making cookies together since she was tiny. When we first started, if I was lucky, most of the ingredients got into the mixing bowl. Her little hands dumped flour around the bowl and all over the floor. But all that could be cleaned up later; the mess was just part of the fun and teaching. As the years have progressed, Christine is the one who makes the cookies. She can read the recipe and measure ingredients all by herself now.

On that particular tea party eve, the kitchen smelled heavenly by the time the cookies emerged from the oven. We all had to sample them while they were still warm to be sure they were good enough for the tea party the next day. They were. Even PaPa gave his approval.

The next morning Christine and Leah woke up to the crowing of Mr. Bibs, our rooster. It was fun for them to race to the coop and let the chickens out for the day. They collected the two eggs Betty had laid and decided to put them into the pancake batter for breakfast. Then, once the breakfast dishes were put away, it was time to get ready for tea.

The girls had elected to have their party in the tree house this year. We asked PaPa to carry the child-sized table and chairs from our loft and place them in the tree house. We all decided a white tablecloth would be appropriate for this special event. Next came the centerpiece. The girls scouted the grounds to find just the right flowers and arranged them in a vase along with a candle.

And then it was time to choose the cups. The year before, I had decided it was time to introduce the girls to my 37-year-old china cup and saucer collection. At the time Bob and I were married, my heart's desire was to have china cups and saucers of my own. So over the years, my Bob, along with family and friends, have given me beautiful china cups and saucers for birthdays and other occasions. Each cup in my collection has special stories and memories. When my mother made her home in heaven in 1980, she left me with her collection of eight special ones.

Four years after that, one of the glass shelves in our hutch collapsed, and many of my cups and saucers shattered. Feeling a little shattered myself, I put the broken pieces in a box and decided to put off dealing with them until a later date.

Finally, six years later—and a few weeks before Christine's tea party—I pulled out the box of broken pieces to see if any cups could be recovered and glued back together. Much to my distress, only one cup and saucer could be repaired—the rest were nothing but tiny pieces.

It was then I realized that the material things we treasure here on earth will one day go "poof." Only that which we treasure in our hearts and spirits will be taken with us—so we do well to put our efforts into making memories and sharing love, not jealously guarding our possessions.

That was when I decided it was time for Christine and Leah to enjoy Grammie's collection. As I led the girls over to the hutch, I began to tell them the stories of the cups and saucers. Then I told them that they could choose any one they wanted for the tea party. I wish you could have seen their eyes as they carefully made their choice of the pattern that appealed to them.

As each girl picked up her cup, I told them, "We must be very careful because these cups and saucers are special and delicate. However, should an accident happen and a cup drop and break—well, that would be unfortunate, but it would be okay. You see, Christine and Leah, you are far more precious to Grammie than the cups and saucers."

Just to ease your mind, those cups and saucers didn't get broken. Those girls placed them very tenderly on the tray with a plate of cookies, fresh, cold, crisp grapes, and a china teapot just waiting for hot cinnamon tea.

However, it was not quite time to sit at their table. First, they needed to get dressed up. To the dress-up box we went, and the girls had a great time helping each other choose an outfit from Grammie's clothes, high heels, hats, gloves, and handbags. Then we trooped to the makeup box. What fun we had decorating those beautiful little faces with lipstick and eye shadow.

Next the dollies were dressed and carried up to the tree house, along with the tea tray. The candle was lit, and we took pictures. What a beautiful setting—and how proud and excited they were! As I walked away and left the girls to their tea, my heart filled with joy and my eyes with tears as I remembered my dear mother pouring tea for her guests in our tiny behind-the-shop apartment.

Those two nine-year-olds chatted and played with the babies for over an hour. The tea was sipped and the cookies and grapes devoured. It was the most beautiful tea party ever—but it won't be the last.

When the girls were finished, the dollies took a nap while the girls took off their clothes and makeup. The aprons went back on, and everything was cleaned up.

Those two little girls learned a lot in 24 hours. They learned how to plan a party and prepare for it, how to set a table, arrange flowers, use good table manners (napkins in laps, small bites, "please" and "thank you"). Most important, they were learning hospitality and experiencing the joy and excitement of sharing their homes and their lives.

Christine's tea parties represent a special bond between the two of us. On Christmas, Christine received her first real china cup and saucer from Grammie Em. It arrived in a special fabric-covered box. I fill that same box every year with something special for Christine. Perhaps, one year, it will hold a teapot, cookie plate, and more cups and saucers...beautiful memories that will never be forgotten by either of us.

I share the tea party story often when I speak, and many woman have told me about china cups and saucers that a grandmother or aunt has given them or passed on to them. One young woman said she had one that her late mother had given her, but it was stored away. She decided to get it out, display it, and share it.

Sharing, you remember, is really what hospitality is all about. To me, the tea party is a catalyst for the kind of sharing that enriches all our lives immeasurably. It's the same experience I had one morning shortly after I lost my precious teacups. I was speaking about hospitality in the state of Washington, and I related my heartbreaking story. The next morning, my hostess served me coffee in a beautiful china cup and saucer from her collection. I enjoyed that thoughtful treat and admired her pattern. Upon leaving and saying our goodbyes, she handed me a wrapped package to open later. Much to my surprise and joy, it was the very cup and saucer I had drunk coffee from that morning! I will never forget her loving, heartfelt gift of hospitality. And whenever anyone chooses her cup from my collection to use, I tell the story behind it. Her willingness to share has become part of the heritage of hospitality I want to pass on to future generations.

Remember, it's not one generation of women we are raising, but many. My mother taught me as I watched her pull her two china cups and saucers from her cupboard and share hospitality with her customers behind our little dress shop. I taught my daughter, Jenny, who entertains so gracefully in her own way, and we are passing on the heritage of hospitality to Christine. One day, I hope, Christine will pass on what she is learning to her own children. That way the blessing of hospitality will continue on through the generations, warming hearts, touching lives, and making home a beautiful place.

Simple Secrets

ॐ You don't have to be a little girl to enjoy a tea party! I love to serve my afternoon guests fragrant cinnamon tea, poured into their choice from my cup and saucer collection, and my wonderful, healthful oatmeal cookies.

ॐ Don't miss the joy of sharing your Christian life through hospitality. Open your home to Bible studies, small group meetings, and after-church fellowships. And don't forget that sharing hospitality is a wonderful way to witness.

❧ Try taking your hospitality on the road. Fill a basket with food and take it to someone who needs encouragement.

❧ Do you know your neighbors? Build a sense of brotherhood in your area by inviting neighbors over for dinner or a snack. Or for a fun event, host a neighborhood barbecue.

❧ A favorite event at our house is a waffle-bar brunch or tea. I serve delicate multigrain waffles with bowls of fresh strawberries, grated coconut, raisins, slivered almonds, real whipping cream, vanilla yogurt, and real maple syrup from Vermont. I've seen ladies in their Sunday best pile up their plates like football players at an after-game party.

❧ Even if you don't have kids, keep a supply of cookies and Popsicles in your freezer and invite neighborhood children over regularly to talk and play.

❧ Many times I place a tiny gift by our dinner guests' plates—a small address book, a pen, nail clippers, a hankie, a powder puff, a pot holder tied with a bow, a dishtowel or dishcloth, or an autographed book. Everyone loves a present.

❧ To get a different angle on the spirit of hospitality, try serving a shift or two in your local soup kitchen or food bank. Better still, volunteer on a regular basis.

❧ If your budget is slim, try hosting a potluck or a theme dinner to which every guest is invited to bring a dish. Or invite six or eight friends to start a "supper club" with you, meeting each month in a different home and contributing dishes to a different menu.

❧ Invest in extra pillows, blankets, and other bedding for overnight guests, and store them in pillowcases to keep them fresh and dust-free.

❧ Try putting an overnight guest in your child's room for the night and give your child the "privilege" of camping out in the living room. The result: an adventure for your child and welcome privacy for your guest.

* One hostess I read about welcomed her overnight guests by placing photos of the two of them—hostess and guest—on the bedside table.

* What aspect of your home or apartment do you enjoy most—the view, the quiet, the yard? Let that aspect be the focus of your hospitality. Share the aspects of your life that bring you pleasure.

* Even if guests elect to stay in a nearby motel, you can extend hospitality with a few special touches. Have a floral arrangement sent to their room. Or leave a basket of homemade muffins at the desk for their arrival.

* When other people extend hospitality to you, don't forget to thank them! A heartfelt note or a little gift will let your hosts know how much you appreciate them. And a return invitation should be not an obligation, but a joy.

Chapter 9

The best laughter, the laughter that can heal, the laughter that has the truest ring, is the laughter that flowers out of a love for life and its Giver.

—MAXINE HANCOCK

The Secret of Celebration

*L*et's party," say the commercials.
And I say "amen!"

Not to loudness and drinking and carousing, of course, but to the kind of celebrations that brighten our everydays and flavor our special times with joy.

The beauty of home is comprised of so many things—order, serenity, creativity, warmth, welcome. But surely the spirit of celebration also adds its special touch—the abiding joy and contagious laughter that say, "I'm glad I'm here. I'm glad you're here. And I'm really glad we're in this together."

Christians, especially, have reason to make the spirit of celebration a trademark of our lives. Tom Sine reminds us:

> We ought to live lives exploding with joy—as though we actually believe that Jesus Christ rose from the dead! We need to be Christmas, Easter, and the kingdom of God all at the same time to the people around us.

Remember, the Bible describes the kingdom again and again with pictures of hilarity, festivity, and celebration. It describes the sumptuous banquet feast of God, the discovery and sharing of lost treasure, the festivity of harvest, the jubilation of the prodigal's party—and, of course, the unspeakable joy of the wedding celebrations of our reigning King.

We're headed for a party to end all parties, so let's start living like it now.[1]

I say "amen" to that too! What a wonderful reason to infuse our homes and our lives with joyful sounds, happy gatherings, and heartfelt smiles...the God-given, life-enhancing secret of celebration.

Celebrating Laughter

Laughter is a definite part of any time of celebration—a gift of God that brightens good days and lightens rough ones. Laughter even has a healing quality to it. People have recovered from serious diseases by learning to laugh each day. Even more people have regained the courage to go on in painful circumstances when they were able to laugh.

Proverbs 17:22 says that a cheerful heart is good medicine. Laughter can draw others to you and lighten your load in life. When you begin to laugh at life and at yourself, you gain new perspective on your struggles. You begin to see a speck of light at the end of the tunnel.

A life without laughter quickly becomes a breeding ground for depression, physical illness, and a critical spirit. But a laughter-filled life unleashes the benefits of celebration.

It's so easy to lose a sense of celebration by taking life too seriously. Bob and I have always said that if we had it to do over again, we would have laughed more. And oh, how I treasure the times we have laughed together!

There is much to laugh about. Cultivate the joy of celebration in your life by looking for "the sillies" in your circumstances.

Our granddaughter, Christine, at seven years of age, called her PaPa to tell him a joke. That began a long ritual between them of telling each other jokes. In fact they each bought a joke book and are still passing funny stories back and forth. Their enjoyment of simple humor makes the rest of us smile too.

Laughter is contagious. I remember a time when our whole family—Bob and I, Jenny and Brad, and their families—shared a vacation. All nine of us got on a plane and flew to Cabo San Lucas, Mexico, for nine days. One late afternoon on the beach, our son-in-law started telling about one of his clients. He continued on and on and for some reason I began to laugh over this poor woman. No one was laughing but me, but I couldn't stop, and soon all nine of us were laughing hysterically on the beach.

> *The highest and most desirable state of the soul is to praise God in celebration for being alive.*
>
> —LUCI SWINDOLL

Even the little children were laughing at Grammie Em's laughing. And the rest of that week, at five in the afternoon, one of the grandchildren would exclaim, "It's time to start laughing"—and we'd all start in again.

When our children were living at home, we always said our family would have been really boring without Jenny because she always gave us reason to lighten up and laugh. Now her son, Chad, lightens our lives with the same mischievous spirit, and his little brother, Bevan, cracks us up with his silly faces.

So cultivate celebration in your life and home by making room for laughter. Deliberately seek it out. Begin today as you smile at someone and find something worth laughing about. As the laughter permeates your life, the spirit of celebration will take root in your heart and you will rediscover the meaning of another proverb: "The cheerful heart has a continual feast" (Proverbs 15:15).

Celebrating Tradition

"Again!"

The toddler giggled with delight as I hid my face once more behind my hands. I giggled too, enjoying the moment of discovery—the instance when my new little granddaughter first began celebrating tradition.

At its simplest level, isn't that why traditions are begun? We experience something good and joyful and meaningful, and we want to do it again. And why not? Repeating our good experiences is one way we begin to learn, to make sense of our lives.

Think how hard our lives would be if we had to invent them all over again every day. Think of all the energy we would waste, all the mistakes we would repeat, all the remembered joy we would lose, all the loneliness we would feel, if we were forced to start from scratch without the ability to say to ourselves, "I like this; this is meaningful—let's do it again."

Tradition is so much more, though, than the simple urge to repeat a pleasant experience. Tradition helps us keep our feet on the ground. It helps us feel the connection between where we have been and where we are going, between those who have gone before us and those who follow after. There's such a comfort, such a sense of relationship, in saying, "This is the way we've always done it."

But there's more. Tradition also helps us understand—and celebrate—who we are and to be thankful for the gift of life and for the people God used to give it to us.

Many wonderful traditions combined to make me who I am, and as I grow older I celebrate more and more my unique heritage.

My father, a Viennese chef, imparted an Old World appreciation for gracious living—fine food, beautiful preparation, and professional excellence (plus some wonderful recipes!). My mother, the daughter of a tailor and the proprietor of a dress shop, taught me to appreciate beautiful fabrics, skillful tailoring, effective organization, and hard work—as well as the importance of making a welcoming home for those I love. Growing up as the American child of an immigrant parent, I inhaled both Old World ambience and New World freedom and opportunity. And I married into wonderful traditions as well—those of a three-generation farm family from Texas.

More important, I am privileged to inherit the richness of two great religious traditions. I grew up in a Jewish home, celebrating the ancient traditions that shaped the earthly heritage of Jesus and his disciples. And then, when my Bob led me to the Lord, I became part of a whole new tradition—2000 years of worship and suffering and celebration and hope. I learned to sing hymns that Christians have sung for centuries, read the same Word that has guided their lives (in various translations), prayed the same prayers, shared the same body and blood. As a Christian, I love the feeling that I'm part of something bigger than I am, a truth that stretches back to creation, a body of believers that spans the generations and the centuries.

Proverbs 24:3-4 says, "By wisdom a house is built, and through understanding it is established; through knowledge its rooms are filled with rare and beautiful treasures."

Traditions are one way that knowledge is passed from generation to generation. They have filled our lives with many "rare and beautiful treasures" over the years, and we have tried to pass those treasures on to our children. We share and celebrate our special ways of doing things, many of which come from the traditions that shaped us.

Celebrating New Traditions

But celebrating tradition isn't just a matter of proceeding in familiar, well-worn paths trodden by those who came before us. Even as we celebrate the past, we should look forward to the future, planning for memories and establishing new traditions that will shape our celebrations for years to come. After all, the memories of tomorrow are being shaped by the traditions we create today.

Bob and I have had such fun establishing traditions in our family. One of the most meaningful began on our first Christmas together—my very first Christmas as a Christian. Money was tight that year, but we managed a tree, and we gave each other ornaments. And we continued to give each other ornaments in the following years. When the children were born, they got ornaments too. (Years later, when Jenny got married at age 22, we gave Jenny and her husband 22 ornaments to start their own tree.)

And the tradition continues as our family grows. Some years ago I decided not to give ornaments; after 33 years I thought nobody cared. How wrong I was! Everybody was so disappointed that I went out first thing on December 26 and found just the right ornaments to continue the tradition. And that practice of giving ornaments, begun by Bob and me on our first Christmas together, still warms our hearts when we gather together year after year.

We already have many beautiful memories of our "You Are Special Today" plate—an old American tradition that is a relatively new one in our family. We often bring this bright red plate out at dinnertime to celebrate special people who sit at our table.

When our grandson Chad was six, he created a new twist to the red plate. We had set it at PaPa Bob's place to honor his birthday. Chad exclaimed, "Let's all go around and tell PaPa why we think he's special." So we did. What a great idea!

The next week the grandchildren came for dinner, and Chad said, "Grammie Em, let's use the special red plate at dinner." I said, "Great! Whom should we honor tonight?" "How about me?" he said. We all honored Chad that evening, and we went around and told Chad how special he was. Then he said, "Now I want to tell you why *I* think I'm special."

This began yet another new tradition for the red plate. It's helped us celebrate how special we are not only to others and ourselves, but also to the Lord, who created us and gave us eternal life. It reminds us that we are sons and daughters of the living God.

Our children were already grown and away from home the year I discovered a beautiful "Christmas memory book" with places to put in photos and write in family memories for every Christmas. "What a great idea!" I exclaimed to Bob. "Too bad we didn't have it 25 years ago." Bob's answer was, "There's nothing wrong with starting now. It's never too late to start a tradition." I'm so glad we did, for that book has given us a wonderful record of how our family has grown and changed since we started keeping it.

Each Christmas since that year, we have made a priority of taking a family photo to put into our book. We write down where we celebrated, who was present, what happened, how we felt. It's become a beautiful collection of holiday memories. It shows who gathered with us each Christmas and where we gathered, and it records special holiday events and memories of the past year.

I look back at the family photo taken that first year. It was just the four of us—Bob and I, Jenny and Brad. Since then we've added a son-in-law and daughter-in-law and grandchildren. Had we not started the tradition, we would never have had such a lovely book of memories.

Recently Bob and I have started the tradition of taking the week after Christmas off to rest and relax and refocus on the coming year. Each year during this time, we write our grown children a letter reflecting back on the past year and expressing our hopes and dreams for the coming year. That's another practice that's fast becoming a meaningful tradition for us.

Traditions add such joy and richness to our lives. But that doesn't mean *all* traditions have to be continued. Should one not meet the needs of your family at the time, don't be afraid to discontinue or modify it.

During our early years as a family, we always reserved Friday evenings for family nights. We would pop corn, play a game, or do something together as a family group. When the children grew older and became active in cheerleading, football, basketball, volleyball, and swim meets (not to mention dating), we changed our family time to Sunday. We would all have breakfast together before church or share brunch after church. Because we were willing to be flexible, our tradition of family time continued until the children were married.

Traditions are meant to enhance our lives, not clutter them or stifle them. In a way traditions are like closets. If you keep on adding new ones and never give up old ones, you end up with overstuffed lives, "wrinkled" observances, and a lot of stress from trying to do too much. But if you keep your priorities straight, your ideas flexible, and your enthusiasm for celebration strong, traditions do nothing but enhance your life.

Celebrate the Seasons

Every season of the year brings with it possibilities for celebration—opportunities to celebrate old traditions and begin new ones, to enjoy each other and the lives God has given us. In fact, that's the purpose of holidays in the first place: to punctuate the year with celebration.

What a tragedy that holidays have become so commercialized and our expectations have climbed so high that getting together with loved ones sometimes brings more stress than enjoyment! It really doesn't have to be that way. When approached with a healthy desire for celebration, holidays can give us something to look forward to. They can be times of love, rest, and refreshment from the daily routine—not a demanding extra that adds to everyone's busy load.

Look over the year—there are so many opportunities for joyful celebration. One fun way to ring in the new year is to set aside a day of food and games. Ask those who received the gift of a game for Christmas to bring it, then divide into groups to play the games. One family I know has developed a New Year's Eve tradition of playing games until midnight, then stopping to celebrate the New Year.

Winter is a great season for celebration, especially if you have snow. Put together a snowman festival, letting teams of two to four people create and dress a snowman (or snowperson). Or try making snow sculptures of family members—even the cat and dog. If you live in a place where winter is warm the way I do, throw an indoor "penguin party" with hot soup, cozy times by the fire, and winter-weather songs—and have fun pretending that it's icy outdoors!

Valentine's Day is packed with possibilities for celebrating the special people in your life. Why not break out the doilies and construction paper to make an old-fashioned valentine for someone special? Or buy some food coloring and heart-shaped cookie cutters and make pink-heart pancakes, heart-shaped French toast, or sweetheart sandwiches for lunch boxes.

Saint Patrick's Day is fun when organized around a green theme. Wear green and eat green—green salad, green Jello, green beans, green cabbage (along with the traditional corned beef).

If your church celebrates Holy Week—Ash Wednesday, Maundy Thursday, Good Friday, Easter Vigil—make a commitment to attend all the services. Or enrich your understanding of God's family by attending services at a church of a different tradition.

For Easter, attend a sunrise service or put together your own family service. Sing praises, read the Easter story, and celebrate the empty tomb. When you think about it, Easter ought to be the biggest celebration of all for Christians. Enjoy it!

Enjoy spring by flying kites, riding bikes, throwing Frisbees, and planning picnics. Have the whole family pitch in to spring clean the house, yard, and/or garage. When you're through, celebrate with pizza or ice cream. Or have a spring tea for all the little girls in the neighborhood and use it as an outreach.

Summer is a great time to celebrate. Go fishing, surfing, or rock climbing. Enjoy beach parties, hot dog roasts, hiking, volleyball games, or croquet. If you live near the coast, hold a neighborhood clambake. If you don't, how about pretending with a clam chowder party?

The Fourth of July and Labor Day provide wonderful, festive opportunities for outdoor celebrations. Why not throw a block party? Close off the street if possible and ask all the neighbors to bring cold cuts, watermelon, ice cream, or other warm-weather goodies. Let the neighbor children decorate their bikes, little cars, ponies, dogs, and themselves to have a neighborhood parade.

Autumn brings golden days that just call out for a celebration. If you have a garden, rediscover an old tradition and invite friends and family over to help you harvest and can and also to help you enjoy the fruits of the harvest.

Halloween, with its pagan history and frightening modern abuses, has become problematic for many Christians these days. But children and adults love the fun of dressing up in costumes and playing games. So why not provide a safe, festive, Christ-centered alternative on October 31 or at another time in the year? Have a yearly costume party to celebrate a birthday, anniversary, holiday, or retirement. Or celebrate All Saints' Day, November 1, by dressing up as biblical people or great Christians of the past.

Thanksgiving is a wonderful time for celebrating the wonderful gifts God has given us. Don't waste it by just stuffing down food. Try to attend special Thanksgiving services or, even better, have one of your own. For almost 20 years we hosted a Thanksgiving service in our home for friends, neighbors, and anyone else who wanted to come. It started when we as a family wanted to begin the day with thanks to God. When the children got a bit older, they wanted to invite their friends. Their parents were intrigued and wanted to come. I would serve hot cider and cinnamon rolls. As the tradition grew, others helped to bring goodies. Our service would begin with a time of singing, and then people would share things they were thankful for. What a beautiful hour we experienced!

And then comes Christmas—such a very special time of celebration. There is so much you can do to celebrate without losing touch with the real cause for celebration, Christ's coming.

Our family has a tradition of reading, as a family, one new book every Christmas. It could be a Christmas story or an Easter story. Other families read the same story every year. Check with your Christian bookstore for a family book of stories.

Involve the whole family in your celebrations. One way to do this is to encourage children to participate in a play or let them perform some other way. Last year at our family Christmas party, one child recited from Luke while the other children acted out the story. Many of us blinked back tears as we watched those children in their makeshift costumes telling the story of Jesus' birth.

Celebrate Each Other

Throughout the year, season to season, times of celebration can help you appreciate the beauty and wonder of the unfolding seasons. All these special days can become calendar reminders to rejoice over the many wonderful gifts God has given us. And when we look at celebration this way, we can see that the most important celebrations of all are the ones that celebrate our love for each other. Birthdays, anniversaries, weddings, and even funerals offer us wonderful opportunities to rejoice over our relationships and express our caring.

Birthdays especially are natural causes for celebration, for they are a time when we gather to celebrate the life of one particular well-loved human being. Birthdays are always "big deals" in our family. The form of the celebration may vary—from a quiet family gathering to a big surprise blowout—but we always have a dinner handpicked by the birthday boy or girl. And we always seek out special ways to make that person feel loved and appreciated.

The same thing goes, of course, for anniversary celebrations. The most meaningful anniversaries are not the most elaborate or the most expensive, but the ones that best commemorate the meaning of the couple's years together. Our friends, Jim and Barbara, recently celebrated their twenty-fifth wedding anniversary. During the event their two sons, David and Jim, took around their video camera and visited all the special people in Jim and Barbara's lives—parents and children, high-school buddies, and new friends. More than 25 people shared fun memories of this wonderful couple. The cutest part was when their adult sons confessed on video to all manner of boyhood escapades that their parents had never found out. What a wonderful way to celebrate a joyous and fruitful marriage!

Celebrations Big and Small

A home can be made beautiful when celebration finds a natural expression in parties and get-togethers, in times of laughter and revelry. But the celebrating spirit need not limit itself to party time. In fact, as Philippians 4:4 tells us, we are to rejoice in the Lord *always*. The spirit of celebration is for all of our lives.

This means that celebration shows itself in little moments of grace as well as in rambunctious revelry. It smiles in a geranium on a sunlit windowsill as well as in a cookout at the beach. It sighs in satisfaction over a humble task done to God's glory and exhilarates over a creative task completed. It glows in an understanding glance as well as in a gala anniversary party. We celebrate because our lives overflow with things to be thankful for, and because God gives us the eyes to see how incredibly we have been blessed.

There are so many ways to celebrate God's gifts of our lives and our relationships—and of himself! We celebrate when we rejoice in beauty and when we work to make our homes beautiful. We celebrate when we take the time to nurture ourselves and our families. We celebrate through our willingness to share, to love each other, to grow. And we celebrate by opening our lives to the Lord and letting his Spirit fill us to overflowing.

I wish for you that spirit of celebration, both little and large, in every corner of your life. I wish you moments of quiet grace and hours of exuberant rejoicing. In your work and your relaxation, in your mealtimes and your bedtimes, in your home and wherever you go, may all your living give you cause for celebration.

And again I say, "amen!"

Simple Secrets

❧ Make laughter a tradition in your family. Tell jokes, clip cartoons, and share funny stories about things that happened to you during the day. Don't overlook opportunities to poke fun at yourself when you make a mistake. Through your example, kids can learn not to take themselves too seriously.

❧ Celebrate your memories. Choose one day a year to gather and look through photo albums, show slides, and watch home videos. (This would be a good time to find homes for loose photos and to catalog the videos too.) Enjoy remembering the past together.

❧ Write mom and/or dad—or whoever was responsible for raising you—a letter about your favorite memories and your favorite traditions your family celebrated when you were a child. Be sure to say thank you!

❧ Let down your hair and play games like tag and hide-and-seek as a whole family. Modify the rules, if you have to, so that all ages can join in—and remember to have fun.

❧ Celebrate your family's cultural heritage—Italian, Scottish, Mexican, Chinese, or American heartland—with a special kind of party. If the food and customs are unfamiliar to you, buy a book or ask an older relative to teach you. Play appropriate music, eat native food, even learn a folk dance while you celebrate a part of your background.

❧ Celebrate somebody else's heritage too! We love putting together a Mexican fiesta complete with spicy food, colorful clothes, and mariachi music. Why not have a piñata for the kids?

❧ One of the best ways to celebrate God's gifts is to share them. Several times a year create a "Love Basket" filled with food for a needy family or the homeless. Or try spending part of your holidays helping out at a local rescue mission.

❧ At your next get-together, have your guests share their favorite family traditions. Write them down and vote for your favorite.

❧ Put together a collection of family photos to brighten a wall or decorate a table. Or why not celebrate a friendship by filling one of those multiphoto frames with snapshots of your times together and giving the montage to your friend?

❧ Celebrate your friendships with other women by throwing an "all girls" party. I love to do this in the spring with tea, fresh flowers, and a lovely brunch, but there are many other possibilities. One pair of unmarried roommates I knew threw a casual party and invited a group of women who didn't know each other. They had a wonderful time getting acquainted and finding out how much they had in common.

❧ Mark the beginning of a new phase of your life—a marriage, a new baby, even a new house—by starting a tradition. One couple I know has their photo taken every year on their anniversary. Their collection now includes formal shots, household portraits, and one quickie snap taken by strangers at a roadside campground.

❧ If you have the right attitude, even mishaps and mistakes can become fun traditions in your family. One family I know turned a birthday cake disaster—one layer of cake sliding off the other— into an occasion for laughter. They just frosted the cake as it was and enjoyed it. After that, something was *always* wrong with the cake—a perfect cake would have been a disappointment.

❧ Give a lift to the spirit of celebration by keeping a list of blessings in your life. Go over the list each morning and remember that you have reason to celebrate every day.

Notes

Chapter 1—The Secret of Welcome

1. Keith Miller and Andrea Wells Miller, *The Single Experience* (Waco: Word, 1981), pp. 30-31.

2. Ibid., p. 31.

Chapter 6—The Secret of Stillness

1. Anne Ortlund, *Disciplines of the Beautiful Woman* (Waco: Word, 1977), p. 29.

Chapter 7—The Secret of Godliness

1. Bonnie Green, "Adultery," in Florence Littauer, *Lives on the Mend* tape series (Waco: Word Educational Products, 1985).

Chapter 9—The Secret of Celebration

1. Tom Sine, *Why Settle for More and Miss the Best?* (Waco: Word, 1987), p. 116.

Other Harvest House Books by Emilie Barnes

Abundance of the Heart

Emilie's Creative Home Organizer

Help Me Trust You, Lord

A Cup of Hope

More Hours in My Day

Keep It Simple for Busy Women

Strength for Today, Bright Hope for Tomorrow

Safe in the Father's Hands

For more information regarding speaking engagements and additional material, please send a self-addressed, stamped envelope to:

More Hours in My Day
2150 Whitestone Drive
Riverside, CA 92506
(909) 682-4714